Therman Sermons

Illuminating The Darkness

Therman Sermons

Illuminating The Darkness

Pastor Therman Russell

Copyright © 2020 Therman Russell

All rights reserved. This book or any portion thereof may not be reproduced or used in any manner whatsoever without the express written permission of the author except for the use of brief quotations in a book review.

ISBN: 979-8-6439-3641-1

Printed by Kindle Direct Publishing

Cover and interior design by Tami Boyce
www.tamiboyce.com

TABLE OF CONTENTS

Preface		vii
Chapter 1	Have a Nice Day	1
Chapter 2	How's Your Friend Faith Doing?	8
Chapter 3	Grace — You Don't Deserve It!	25
Chapter 4	How Do You Plead? Guilty or Not Guilty?	52
Chapter 5	I Agree With That	61
Chapter 6	I Just Wanna Be Myself!	74
Chapter 7	I Just Don't Believe!	88
Chapter 8	What Ails You?	94
Chapter 9	Wisdom	102
Chapter 10	"Free at last, Free at Last..."	109
Chapter 11	Managing Your Expectations	118
Chapter 12	The Language of Success	135
Chapter 13	Flesh and Spirit	143
Chapter 14	Fear - The Purpose Killer	160
Chapter 15	My Flesh is Not My Friend!	170
Chapter 16	A Message to the Self-Righteous	192
Chapter 17	That's All Folks!	217

PREFACE

I hope you find this book to be of some value to you; however, it would be of even greater value if you, at some point in your life (if you haven't already) make the personal choice to believe in the existence of God (the Father), Jesus Christ (the Son and saviour of humanity), and the Holy Spirit (whom we invite to live in us). These three are one (The Holy Trinity).

I say, "Make the personal choice" because if you've ever felt obliged, or forced to believe in God because of cultural or family traditions, pressure or demands placed on you by society, or by any other non-voluntary circumstances; then that's not belief at all; instead, it's just you going along with the program for fear of consequences.

Believing in God is, has always been, and must always be a personal choice; an act of an individual's free will. If you aren't already a believer, the intention of this book is not to convert you (whether you believe or not is entirely up to you); my prayer is that as a result of reading this book, you will have the truth and understanding necessary to make the choice to believe.

This book is not just for Christians, but for anyone and everyone. My desire is that it will in some way help lift the fog of confusion, misconception, and contradiction people's religious agenda casts over God's relationship with you, and your relationship with God. My hope is to show you how God really sees you, and how He sees humanity as a whole.

For Ricky, Susie, Johnny, Eric, Melvin, Leon and Ann

The only people who refuse to address injustice, are those who profit from it.

CHAPTER 1

Have a Nice Day

If there was ever a time where we require truth, clarity of thought, and clarity of mind; it's most certainly now! As we consider or examine our lives, the lives of loved ones and people around us, and the occurrences in the world at large (both man-made, natural and supernatural); it appears that there is more to be concerned and anxious about than there is reason to rejoice; however, this is a false perception.

About eight years before I started writing this book; I decided never to have a bad day again. Yes, I said, "Never" and "I decided"! It's my hope that the content within this book (starting with this chapter), will help you realise how easy it is to choose victory in every situation and circumstance; rather than failure and defeat. Am I implying that victory is a choice? Absolutely! Does that mean you will always have a good day? Well, read on and judge for yourself. I believe this book will reveal that the choice truly is yours; however, it's my sincere desire that you not just read this book for the sake of reading it, but you will instead read it with the expectation of it changing your life for the better; which of course will have a profoundly positive impact not just on you, but on everyone within your circle of influence.

Before we do anything else, we must establish a solid foundation on which to build our defences against a world filled with destructive forces (in many forms); designed specifically to rob us daily of our joy, peace, and victory. You ready? Let's go then!

Does anyone really choose to have trouble in their daily lives? Do we look at pain and suffering and say "Ahh yes, I'll have some of that please"? Do we, with intentional forethought, invite misfortune and mishap into our lives? Well, unless you love pain and misery, or simply have a death-wish; then I'd say no, we don't. We all want to have a good day; don't we? Then I challenge you to *choose* to have a good day. There you go! Simple! The end! Short book! Thank you for reading it!

Okay, okay, I hear you saying, "Hold on there Mr Clever Pants! What do you mean 'choose' to have a good day?!" Well, I meant exactly what I said. Now does this mean that (so called) bad stuff won't happen in any given day? No; however, it all depends on how you react to it! It really is quite that simple.

Tell me, what is it then; do you think you have some sort of responsibility, or obligation to react in a negative and debilitating way when troubles come knocking? Who told you that you do? Who told you that when troubles come, you have to cry, and be afraid, and become weak, indecisive and feeble? To whom do you owe this debt of misery?! If the answer is "No one"; then why do you choose to respond in this way? Why not choose to respond in a way that is more likely to allow you to navigate through the situation, or circumstances, in such a way that will not have an adverse, debilitating, or (at worst) destructive effect on yourself, or a loved one, or anyone else for that matter? Think about it.

I've been driving for many years and I've had my share of close calls on the roads; however, what I've discovered is that when they've occurred I, in that moment, become very calm and focused and I manoeuvre my way out of trouble. I could be in mid-sentence, talking to my wife in the passenger seat and manoeuvre my way out of an unanticipated, dangerous situation without dropping a word; no rise in heart beat or blood pressure, no frayed nerves, and especially no rage. I just calmly manoeuvre my way out of the crisis, my day goes on, and that incident isn't even a blip on my radar. So, what am I saying? The way I respond to a close call on the road is a choice, my choice. I literally choose to respond in a way that would give me the best opportunity to achieve a positive outcome, and keep my day stress free.

I've embraced this revelation of our ability to choose how we respond, when life throws us a wobbly, and I apply it to every single circumstance and situation in my life! The good news is: so can you! How you respond to the things you face in life is a choice, YOUR choice.

Does this mean I never get angry or raise my voice? No. It means that if I do get angry or raise my voice; it is necessary to do so, to bring about a positive outcome. In other words; an anger that is not motivated by malice, resentment, hate, or any other negative spirit, but instead; a righteous anger - righteous indignation. For example: the anger I display when I see injustice in the world (in its many forms) is righteous indignation. The anger Jesus projected towards the money changers and vendors, at the temple (John 2:13-16), was righteous indignation. Don't get me wrong, I don't expect you to walk around whistling, with your head in the clouds, whilst everything around you is crumbling, no; sometimes you have to fight for your peace, your joy, your victory;

however, the "fight" is motivated by righteous indignation, and not malice.

James 4:7 (King James Version) "Submit yourselves therefore to God. Resist the devil, and he will flee from you." Responding to hardships and challenges in the way described in this chapter is one of the ways you resist the devil, and as you submit yourself before God; suddenly you'll find that challenges become fewer and fewer, to the point where you'll no longer acknowledge them as "challenges", but as opportunities to be strengthened in your character, and in your faith.

So, let your response to (so called) troubles be contrary to how people would expect you to respond, or behave; no exceptions - not even death! "Did he just say, not even death?!" Yes, he did! ***1 Corinthians 15:54-55 (KJV) [54] "So when this corruptible shall have put on incorruption, and this mortal shall have put on immortality, then shall be brought to pass the saying that is written, Death is swallowed up in victory. [55] O death, where is thy sting? O grave, where is thy victory?"*** Like I said; to whom do you owe a debt of misery?!

Choosing to have a good day, by responding positively to life's curve balls, is the foundation on which we are able to establish firm spiritual footing; giving us the ability to see beyond seeing, and to hear beyond hearing; which are the very attributes we require if we are to navigate joyously through the labyrinth of life. Will this be easy? Let's be real, no; because you're used to responding to "troubles" in the way you think, or (even worse) the way other people "think" you should; nonetheless, I challenge you to practice this every day, with consistency, and watch how it will change your life!

*You shall have what you expect —
good or bad; you shall have
what you expect.*

CHAPTER 2

How's Your Friend Faith Doing?

How do you define faith? How do you know if you have faith? Is it possible to have faith for some things and not for others? How do you acquire faith, and maintain it? These are all questions I will attempt to answer in this chapter, with the hope that you will never be in doubt as to anything concerning the provisions you have access to, through God's divine grace.

Let me start by saying that the actions you take in response to what you "say" you believe, or expect; is what determines whether you really believe or are really expecting it. In other words; your actions determine whether you really have faith or not. ***James 2:15-17 (Amplified Version) [15] "If a brother or sister is poorly clad and lacks food for each day, [16] And one of you says to him, Good-bye! Keep yourself warm and well fed, without giving him the necessities for the body, what good does that do? [17] So also faith, if it does not have works (deeds and actions of obedience to back it up), by itself is destitute of power (inoperative, dead)."*** What are you doing in response to what you "say" you believe? Now before you go off on a tangent of "Namin' and Claimin'!", "Blabbin' and Grabbin'!"; please remember that what you say you believe, or are expecting, must be consistent with what God desires for you; otherwise, it's just you going off on...well, a tangent!

Through the sacrifice of Jesus Christ, God has made a new covenant with humanity; a covenant of grace, which includes forgiveness. Through this covenant of grace, we have access to many wonderful things provided to make our existence here on earth truly meaningful, helpful to others, and completely and utterly fulfilling in every way. How we respond; however, to the promises in this new covenant, determines whether they will be effective in our lives or not. A person says, "I heard and I believe that if I cross this road, I will make it to the other side."; but the person never takes action by crossing the road! Another person says, "I heard and I believe that if I cross this road, I will make it to the other side."; then he or she crosses the road. Which person has faith? It's a simple analogy; but you get my point. Now apply this principal to everything the new covenant of grace entitles you to, and ask yourself; how are you responding to it? What are your actions in response to what you say you believe God wants for you? Let me suggest that you at least start by believing in the gospel of grace, and all that it entitles you to; then, as God's desires for you in a given situation become clear; solidify your faith in that situation by your actions.

Hebrews 11:1 (KJV) "Now faith is the substance of things hoped for, the evidence of things not seen." Firstly, we must establish that God is the author of faith. It is only by God's definition that we understand what faith really is. I say this because "faith" is a word that is often used without really understanding its true meaning. So, before we even talk about whether you have faith or not; I thought it just might be a good idea to first agree on its true definition: "The substance of things hoped for, the evidence of things not seen." Words like "substance" and "evidence" are used to describe something tangible. So faith is the thing that makes what we hope for, tangible (real).

If you really understand the true meaning of faith; then you'll know that the thing you hope for becomes real not when you see it, but at the very moment you have faith for it! "Then why doesn't it instantly materialise at the time I have faith for it?!" (I hear you say.) One word: "Timing"! ***James 1:3 (Amp) "Be assured and understand that the trial and proving of your faith bring out endurance and steadfastness and patience."*** If you will wait on Him, in some instances, if it's His will, God will use the time between the activation of your faith, and you seeing the physical manifestation in the here and now; to mould and strengthen your character. The problem is, many people misunderstand what it means to "wait". So how do you know if you're truly waiting? Well here's a clue: the "waiting" is supposed to strengthen your character, so if whilst you're "waiting", you're freaking out with anxiety, fear, anger, resentment, and so on; the only thing that's likely to do is make you ill; it certainly won't strengthen your character! Now; on the other hand, if your mind is at peace, and your countenance restful, in spite of all hell breaking loose around you; then you are waiting in the true sense of the word, and that will most certainly make you stronger!

Moving on. Now, where was I? Oh yeah...

Don't get me wrong; it is possible of course, to acquire stuff without God's direct help, or approval. Humans are powerful beings, created in the image of God, we can do anything. However, show me a person who has acquired much, without acknowledging God in his or her life, and I'll show you a person who is bereft of wisdom, and shallow in depth of character. (Ouch!) Amongst other things this person would be self-serving, and would find it impossible to act altruistically. (Ouch again!) **Mark 8:36 (KJV)** *"For what shall it profit a man, if he shall gain the whole world, and lose his own soul?"*

"Self-serving?! How dare you!" Let's face it, if you're not surrendered to Jesus, the embodiment of purity, goodness, grace, and unconditional love, who are you serving? By what measure do you determine the integrity of your actions; even your character and honour? By what measure do you determine the true motives behind your acquisition of substance and wealth? By your family member? By your friend? By your neighbor? By me? We're all just as broken as you are! Jesus; however, is perfect in all His ways, and when we measure our thoughts, words, actions, character, and our motives by His righteousness; we acquire the means by which we may truly be great, and do great things; not for our glory, but for the benefit of others, to God's glory! Forgive me for going on a rant; but this needed addressing.

Now, back to the question of how to know if you have faith: Let's say you're believing for something, and the next day you start to think about a whole bunch of stuff that could happen that would prevent the materialisation (or manifestation if you like) of what you're believing for - you are now doubting. You cannot have doubt and faith for something at the same time, and expect to receive from God. *James 1:5-8 (KJV) [5] "If any of you lack wisdom, let him ask of God, that giveth to all men liberally, and upbraideth not; and it shall be given him. [6] But let him ask in faith, nothing wavering. For he that wavereth is like a wave of the sea driven with the wind and tossed. [7] For let not that man think that he shall receive any thing of the Lord. [8] A double minded man is unstable in all his ways."* Fear of not receiving what you are hoping for is called doubt, and doubt cancels faith. One day you have faith, the next day you have doubt, the next day faith, the next day doubt! In the spirit realm, your stuff will be appearing and disappearing like flashing Christmas lights! The angels will be like, "Dude, make up your mind!" When you no longer struggle with doubt, you will know that your faith is intact, and fully functional.

On the question of whether it's possible to have faith for one thing, and not for another; the answer to that is yes, most definitely. 1 Kings 18:18-39 tells us how Elijah's faith caused God to send down fire from the sky to consume the alter of offerings, in order to prove to the people of Israel that He was God. Elijah's faith also allowed him to slay four hundred and fifty false prophets, who were deceiving the people of Israel. By contrast, later, when Elijah had heard that Jezebel was seeking to kill him, he ran for his life (1 Kings 19:1-4); full of fear and weariness, and saying to God that he'd had enough!

It is possible to get to the point where you've had to use your faith so many times, and in so many battles, that you just get tired; however, giving up should never be an option. Why go through all those troubles only to give up?! Why run twenty-five miles of a marathon, only to give up on mile twenty-six?! The same faith that gave you your past victories, is the same faith that will get you through the next one, and the next one, and the next one; until you go home to be with God. We are not promised a life without trials; however, trials are only painful when we don't trust and believe - it's that simple.

Finally, how do you acquire faith, and how do you maintain it? ***Hebrews 11:6 (KJV) "But without faith it is impossible to please Him: for he that cometh to God must believe that He is, and that He is a rewarder of them that diligently seek Him."*** God is not angry with you if you don't have faith. He is; rather, more like a parent who's heartbroken when their child who has left home suffers needlessly, when the child could enjoy having access to all that the parent has provided. It is God's desire for all of humanity to do well; therefore, He is not angry with you for not having faith, it just (to use a human term) breaks His heart.

How's Your Friend Faith Doing?

No one can force you to have faith, faith is a choice; you choose to have faith. Faith is the absence of fear or doubt in relationship to a situation, circumstance, or need, and it is the bridge which gives you access to everything God has provided for you through His grace (by God's definition, "grace" is unearned, unmerited, or undeserved favour).

Now that you know what faith is, you can choose to have it or you can choose not to have it. Acquiring faith is the easy part, it's simply a choice; maintaining or keeping your faith is the challenging part!

Every day, we are exposed to things that can rob us of our faith, for example: news reports, programs we watch, what people say to us, our own conversations with people, the things we do, the things we speak out, the things that happen to us, the things we say to or do to other people, and the list goes on and on. Whatever you are exposed to during the course of your day, will influence your thinking; either to your benefit, or to your detriment; therefore, it is crucial that you think about what you're thinking about.

What do I mean by, "Think about what you're thinking about"? From your very first waking moment, and throughout your entire day; it is very important that you are conscious of how you (or someone else) may be affected by your thoughts, in response to; the things you see, the things you say, what you hear other people say, what you do, what other people do, or any other situations or circumstances that may occur. For instance: Do you wake up in the morning, look out the window, see that it's raining, and say, "Oh what a miserable day." Is that a good way to start your day? Declaring that it's miserable?! Starting your day with a negative statement like that (when there are things you could be grateful for), weakens your defences against other negative thoughts; making you more vulnerable to the negative spirit of doubt. Be aware; therefore, throughout your day, of the things (including your own thoughts) that hinder your faith, as well as the things that strengthen your faith, and seek to avoid those things (including thoughts) that hinder your faith. This requires you to think about what you're thinking about!

The things (mental or physical) that can rob you of your faith can be very subtle, so you really have to be switched on. Any thoughts, emotions, or actions that contradict or conflict with your faith in God, and all His provisions for you, should be recognised immediately, and responded to in such a way so that your faith remains intact. This may require you to avoid some people, or stop listening to, reading or watching some things; however, more than anything, it requires that you be honest with yourself about what is truly good or bad for you with regards to maintaining your faith. If you cannot clearly, sincerely and honestly justify why a particular thing is good for you; then simply avoid it. This really does require honesty and strong character, but it's your call; remember, faith is a choice, and you have to choose to protect it.

Here's a little tip to help you avoid wavering between faith and doubt: Seek the will of God for your life in accordance with God's grace, as outlined in the scriptures of the Bible (which includes mental, emotional, physical and spiritual needs), and ask God for the wisdom to know what to ask for. In other words, read the Bible and pray; asking the Holy Spirit to help you to understand God's true desire for you in that situation, circumstance, or need. When you know that the thing that you're asking for is simply what God has already provisioned for you to have; then you will have confidence in your request, faith is activated, and doubt cannot take hold. This doesn't mean that doubt won't present itself; however, it won't take hold, and you don't lose out. So, if doubt tries to creep into your mind, just reject it; remember what God says about that matter, and simply don't let doubt take it from you.

God is merciful and gracious, trials will come; however, as long as you continue to earnestly seek His presence in your life, God will keep you from being utterly cast down (Psalm 37:24); nonetheless, like a child being raised by a loving and caring parent; it is God's desire (the ultimate parent) that you eventually grow up in Him (spiritually), and operate through Him with wisdom and power. So don't worry, God's got your back through every leg of your life's journey.

Mark 9:24 (KJV) "And straightway the father of the child cried out, and said with tears, Lord, I believe; help thou mine unbelief." Many people use Mark 9:24 to suggest that it's okay if we're not able to have faith in God concerning all things, and that God will help us have faith, or even give us faith. That's not true. The trials you face in life are your opportunities to have faith; however, even then, the choice is yours. Jesus helped this man because the man showed faith by simply asking Jesus to help his son in the first place! The man believed Jesus could do it; that's why Jesus did it! The other reason why Jesus did it was for a demonstration of the power, mercy, and the grace of God; for the benefit of the crowd of people that had gathered.

"I believe, help thou my unbelief." The man was saying, "I believe you can do this Jesus; but help my faith to be complete concerning everything else (all things), so that there is no unbelief in me at all!" Jesus had already said to the man (Mark 9:23), that if he could get to the state where he simply believed (period) not only would this be possible, but so would anything and everything else! Jesus did not say, okay no problem, I'll help you with that, here's some faith, bam! Please note: GOD DOES NOT, AND WILL NOT GIVE YOU FAITH! That's on you!

It is expected of you to believe God all by yourself! When troubles or a bad report comes your way or when things don't seem to be panning out in accordance with God's will for you; that's your opportunity to have faith in God (no matter what) and believe God's report. Does this mean that everything you have faith for will happen? Yes, if it is the will of God; then absolutely! When it doesn't happen, you have to ask yourself, "Was it faith or was it presumption? Was I truly asking according to God's will or not?" Only you and God will know the true answer to that.

We all possess faith in measure, and not in totality; however, total faith is the goal towards which we press. ***Ephesians 3:20 (KJV) "Now unto him that is able to do exceeding abundantly above all that we ask or think, according to the power that worketh in us..."*** This scripture says, "According to the power that works in us." God can do "exceeding abundantly..."; but it's according to the measure of His power at work in us, that "power" that we receive by faith; a faith that is a continuous work in progress to become complete concerning all things.

Complete and total faith as a "work in progress", is not to be confused with double-mindedness. A double-minded person say they believe God; but is fearful. They say they believe; but as soon as they're confronted with something that appears to challenge what they say they're believing

God for; they then become fearful. This was the case with the "giants" in the land of Canaan (Numbers chapter 13), a land God promised to the people of Israel. From fear comes resentment, bitterness and anger, which ultimately affects the person's attitude and behaviour in a myriad of faith cancelling ways. The scriptures (James 1:5-8) speak of people like this, saying that they are unstable in all their ways, and should expect to receive nothing from God.

Numbers, Chapter 14, is a good illustration of how double-minded people can behave, and God's response (in this case) to their double-mindedness which unfortunately, for them, resulted in severe consequences - that's right; they died! Never to have seen the promised land! We all have fallen into the trap of double-mindedness at some time or another, which makes it too serious to ignore; because your moment of double-mindedness could come at a critical time, and could even be a matter of life or death!

So how do you prevent yourself from being double minded? You simply have to know what is God's will for you in that situation, and what isn't! How do you find out what God's will is for you in any given situation? By having a personal relationship with God through accepting the salvation of Jesus Christ, and inviting the Holy Spirit to live within you. Further supported by studying and meditating in God's Word (the Bible), and strengthened by prayer and fasting, sharpened by fellowship with like-minded people, and encouraged and confirmed through the preached Word from ministers of the gospel of whom you are confident are anointed by God to preach truth. Seems like a lot? Not if you're serious about walking in total faith!

Still on the subject of double mindedness, here's an example: I'm at a funeral, and everyone's grieving for their loss. Just because I know that I have faith, and with that faith could bring that person back to life; I wouldn't arbitrarily go up to the coffin, touch the dead body and expect it to come back to life! I personally, would have to know that it's God's will for that person to be brought back to life! I wouldn't think, "Oh, people are crying so I guess I should help out by bringing that person back to life!" No! People die! That's the cycle of life! Instead, I would be thinking, "Father, what is your will in this moment, in this situation, and if God we're to say to me, "Therman, command life to return to that body!"; then I absolutely would! That behaviour doesn't make me double-minded; however, if I've seen the grace, mercy, favour and the power of God demonstrated in my life over and over and over again (as did the people of Israel, spoken of in Numbers chapter 13), and God makes it clear to me that there is something He wants me to have, or something He wants me to do, or I ask God for something that I know is His will for me, and the answer is delayed, or I face adversity whilst waiting; if I then become anxious, fearful, angry, bitter or resentful, that would make me double-minded, and I cannot expect to receive from God that which was asked or promised.

One more thing about faith. Whatever you're asking God for where two or more people are involved in the asking; then spiritual agreement becomes necessary for faith to work; not just faith alone. I cover "agreement" more thoroughly in chapter 5, but here's a taster.

Matthew 18:19-20 (KJV) [19] "Again I say unto you, That if two of you shall agree on earth as touching any thing that they shall ask, it shall be done for them of my Father which is in heaven. [20] For where two or three are gathered together in my name, there am I in the midst of them." "As touching" means "regarding" or "with regards to". There are also two more things that need dissecting here, which is: what it means to "agree", and what it means to be "gathered in my name".

Let's say, on a given day, there's an absolutely huge lottery jackpot. Have you ever said, or thought to yourself, how much you would like to win it? Well guess what; so has your neighbour, and possibly millions of other people! When the numbers are drawn, do you all win the jackpot? I think I can safely say, "Uh, nah!". Wanting the same things does not put you in agreement with someone else. What Jesus is referring to when He says "agree" in verse 19, is spiritual agreement (which I discuss in detail in chapter 5), and where Jesus says (in verse 20), "For where two or three are gathered in my name...", He's talking about the exact same thing, spiritual agreement! In verse 20, Jesus is simply elaborating on what He means by the word "agree" in verse 19!

The "agreement" Jesus is referring to does not mean wanting the same things, it means all parties concerned being connected (meaning in harmony) in Christ; in spirit and in truth, so that the prayers (the "asking") of all parties concerned, are not motivated by their flesh (their fallen nature), but by Jesus, the Holy Spirit, God; who are all one and the same. Spiritual agreement (as I just briefly defined), not just faith on its own, is what gets results when two or more people are (specifically) involved in the asking.

Final thoughts on this, you don't need two or more people to be in spiritual agreement to have faith for your salvation, and you don't have to ask God for your salvation because salvation has already been given. You just simply have to accept by faith (all by yourself) that Jesus was sacrificed, so that humanity could be redeemed for our sins (the byproduct of our corrupt nature); that we may regain access to all that God has intended for us to have, which includes eternal life with Him, in heaven, after our bodies cease to function here on earth.

With people, you are defined by what you do. With God, you are defined by what Jesus did.

CHAPTER 3

Grace — You Don't Deserve It!

Having accepted God's salvation through Jesus Christ, and being baptised at the age of twelve, I've had a connection in some way or another with God from my youth; however, it wasn't until I was twenty-eight that I had my first true revelation of God's existence, and His presence in my life. The revelation (or vision) lasted only a fraction of a second; however, in that tiny moment, God showed me how He sees me, but let me make a few things plain before I continue with my personal testimony.

God created humans in His own image. "Hold on a minute! You're going back to the beginning of time to tell me your testimony?!" I know you're thinking this; however, indulge me for a moment; this is important. The first two humans (Adam and Eve) had (in portion) the glory, power, and authority of God; which included immortality. Think about it, they weren't like humans today; such was the perfection of their pureness, power and glory; that they had the ability to communicate with animals, and have direct, two-way dialogue with God himself! Sadly, all of this was lost when Adam and Eve disobeyed God. By the way, just a foot note here: It was Eve who first (disobediently) ate of the forbidden tree; however, when God asked Adam why he ate from the forbidden tree; Adam replied, **"The woman whom You gave to be with me, she gave me fruit from the tree, and I ate." (Genesis 3:12)** Sorry, but I think this is so funny! I can see Adam now, eyes wide with terror, like a child caught with his hand in the cookie jar; crumbs still around his mouth, "Errr...uhh... Eve made me do it?! Hilarious!! Anyway, where was I...Oh yeah...After this act of disobedience, Adam and Eve's direct connection to God was severed; they also lost their immortality. Unfortunately, this now applied to everyone born after Adam (which is all of humanity) for eternity! Bummer!!

So, what did Adam do that caused him to mess it up for the rest of us?! He let Eve, his wife, talk him into eating fruit from the forbidden tree which was the Tree Of Knowledge Of Good And Evil, which God had clearly forbade them. ***Genesis 2:17 (KJV) "But of the tree of the knowledge of good and evil, thou shalt not eat of it: for in the day that thou eatest thereof thou shalt surely die."*** Meaning they will no longer be immortal. Nonetheless, Adam was obviously thinking, "Happy wife, happy life." so he did what Eve told him to do!

Prior to their disobedience, Adam and Eve had no knowledge of evil, but God knew that once humans gained the knowledge of evil, we would be forever corrupted, because although we're made in the image of God, and being gods ourselves; yes, I said we are gods; that's with a little "g". ***Psalm 82:6-7 (KJV) [6] "I have said, Ye are gods; and all of you are children of the most High. [7] But ye shall die like men, and fall like one of the princes."*** This is spoken again in the New Testament: ***John 10:34 (KJV) "Jesus answered them, Is it not written in your law, I said, Ye are gods?"*** However, we lack the ability to know of evil, and not be corrupted by it. Yes, we (humanity) are gods, but we have been made a little lower than the angels: ***Psalm 8:4-5 (KJV) [4] "What is man, that thou art mindful of him? and the son of man, that thou visitest him? [5] For thou hast made him a little lower than the angels, and hast crowned him with glory and honour."*** This variance between God, the creator, and man, the created, was enough to prohibit us from being incorruptible; hence God kept the knowledge of evil from us.

"I'm not corrupt, I'm a good person!" I hear you say, well, have you ever had a bad thought? Just a little, itty, bitty one? Boom! You're corrupt! The problem is, people compare themselves to other people; however, since we are created in the image of God; God compares us to Himself! So, compared to God, are we good? No, and God created the Old Testament Laws in the Bible to show us just how far we've fallen from our former glorious state; prior to Adam and Eve's disobedience.

How do the laws in the Bible show us how corrupt we are? Because (for one) you'd have to be absolutely perfect to be able to keep (obey) them! It would take a person with our former pureness, glory and power to fulfil the Law of God; however, our former perfect state was sadly lost because of the disobedience of Adam and Eve; but cheer up, all is not lost! In comes Jesus with his bad self...I mean his "good" bad self...aww you know what I mean! God, in the form of the Holy Spirit supernaturally planted a seed of life into the virgin girl, Mary, and Mary gave birth to Jesus. So Jesus was fully human, but also a man who happened to be the son of God, and part of the God Trinity (God the Father, God the Son and God the Holy Spirit). Essentially, God created a new "Adam" (Jesus), the difference being, this "Adam" had the knowledge of both good and evil; but was able to resist the temptations of evil and thereby, was incorruptible. *John 1:1 (KJV) "In the beginning was the Word, and the Word was with God, and the Word was God."*

John 1:14-17 (KJV) [14] "And the Word was made flesh, and dwelt among us, (and we beheld His glory, the glory as of the only begotten of the Father,) full of grace and truth. [15] John bare witness of Him, and cried, saying, This was He of whom I spake, He that cometh after me is preferred before me: for He was before me. [16] And of His fulness have all we received, and grace for grace. [17] For the law was given by Moses, but grace and truth came by Jesus Christ."

Jesus is the Word of God made flesh; carrying all the power and authority of God, which means the Laws of God (His Word) is fulfilled in Jesus. You still following me? Okay, let me make it clearer: By "Laws", I mean the, "Thou shall, thou shall not, must not, will not, touch not, taste not..." and so on. In other words, all the things we were commanded to do (or not to do) so that we may gain favour with God, as well as atone for our fallen nature (our sins).

The "Word" (which includes the complete Law of God) was made flesh in the form of Jesus. So, when Jesus (the Word of God in the flesh) was crucified; so was the Law with him. The Law (or Laws) of God were fulfilled by the sinless, incorruptible life of Jesus Christ; then completely abolished when Jesus carried them with him to the cross. The Law, which condemned us by showing us how far we'd fallen from the glory of our former state; was crucified (killed) on the cross with Jesus, thereby releasing humanity from the Law. ***Colossians 2:14 (Amp) "Having cancelled and blotted out and wiped away the handwriting of the note (bond) with its legal decrees and demands which was in force and stood against us (hostile to us). This note with its regulations, decrees, and demands He set aside and cleared completely out of our way by nailing it to His cross."***

To put it another way, God himself in the form of Jesus took the blame for our sinful nature, and because the penalty for sin is death (Rom 6:23), He (Jesus) died on our behalf. Now here's the clincher, and it's pretty clever: Jesus paid the price of death for the sins of humanity (past, present and future); however, He Himself was sinless, so the realm (which we call hell) that God created for Lucifer (the angel who wanted to "dethrone" God, a.k.a. Satan) and the angels that sided with Lucifer (who were all cast out of heaven), could not keep the spirit of Jesus because the spirit of Jesus is pure and righteous; none other than the Holy Spirit!

Are you getting this?! Because I smell smoke! Come on, stay with me! The Holy Spirit is absolutely pure and cannot sin, so all Jesus did was carry our sins to hell like a delivery man. I can see Jesus now, "Special delivery for Satan!",

Jesus hands Satan our sins, and Satan says, "Ah-ha, I got you Jesus! Now you have to stay in hell with me!" Jesus: "Uh, no I don't!", and flashes His righteous Holy Spirit gold badge - Bam!! Jesus: "In fact, I'm taking you as MY prisoner! ***Ephesians 4:8 (Amp) "Therefore it is said, When He ascended on high, He led captivity captive (He led a train of vanquished foes) and He bestowed gifts on men."***

Colossians 2:15 (Amp) "God disarmed the principalities and powers that were ranged against us and made a bold display and public example of them, in triumphing over them in Him and in it (the cross)." Through Jesus Christ (for all of us who accept His sacrifice), we have authority over all the power of Satan: ***Luke 10:19 (KJV) "Behold, I give unto you power to tread on serpents and scorpions, and over all the power of the enemy, and nothing shall by any means hurt you."***; but that's a whole chapter by itself.

The Bible says in Romans 5:12, **Wherefore, as by one man (Adam) sin entered into the world, and death by sin; and so death passed upon all men, for that all have sinned.** And in Romans 5:19, **For as by one man's disobedience (again, Adam) many were made sinners, so by the obedience of one (Jesus) shall many be made righteous.** So Jesus' sinless life was the qualitative factor in him being a sacrifice for all humanity; dying so that we wouldn't have to die (our spirit that is). Our bodies will cease to function;

however, because of Jesus, (for those who accept Him) our spirit will live on for eternity.

Now, back to my personal testimony. (You thought I forgot; didn't you?) As I said earlier, in a brief fraction of a second, I had a glimpse of how God sees me. I mean this came out of nowhere! I was happily minding my own business. I wasn't sad, or lonely; I wasn't down and out, desperate or depressed; in fact, I wasn't even thinking about God! It just happened! Bam!!

Before my profound revelation, I used to look at the Christians that I knew, and expected them to be the shining example of love, purity and light; only to be sadly disappointed in one way or another, by their behaviour. Eventually I resigned to the attitude that, if these people represent what Christians should be; then I don't want to know! I never; however, lost hope that perhaps one day, all would be revealed, and I'd know the truth about God and His relationship with me and humanity as a whole. So even though I was happily living large, partying hard, smokin' and jokin'; my "radar" for the true living God, was never really switched off. So the day God gave me just a glimpse of who I am in His eyes (how He actually sees me), was the day that changed my life forever, and set me on a mission to find truth. Fast-forward; that mission led me to understanding the grace of God. Grace, meaning unmerited favour, which by definition means I don't deserve it.

All those Christians that I knew, that were (in my opinion) behaving badly; God wasn't moved one bit by it at all! I mean, we're flawed humans, all of us; bad behaviour is our default setting! That's why we need God's grace! What did you or I do to deserve for someone to take the blame, and die for our sinful nature? Nothing! In fact, the Bible says in Romans 5:8 (Amp), ***"But God shows and clearly proves His own love for us by the fact that while we were still sinners, Christ (the Messiah, the Anointed One) died for us."*** So God did not require us to sort out our mess before He forgave us; He just forgave us! Period!!

God knew that we had absolutely no chance of fulfilling to the letter, the requirements set out in Law, which, if we did, would allow us to be restored to our former glory; as in the days of Adam (before the fall). So God sent Jesus to fulfil the Law for us! That's a demonstration of God's grace, because we did absolutely nothing to earn it! So now, when we accept that Jesus paid the price for our sinful nature; through Him, we are restored to our former glory; not in the natural, but spiritually.

I say you don't deserve grace to make a point; but check this out: Once you've accepted God's forgiveness through Jesus Christ, you are entitled to the grace of God, not because of what you've done, but because of what Jesus did! What Jesus did, entitles you to receive all the good things (in the spirit and in the natural) God has purposed for you.

When God showed me how He sees me, He was revealing to me that He looks at me through the "lens" of the sacrifice of Jesus Christ. Even though I was living a wild and crazy life, I (at a certain point in my life) accepted God's forgiveness through Jesus Christ, so from that moment forward till now, all God sees is my righteousness, which has been imputed to me by my faith in the sacrifice of Jesus Christ; no matter how I behave, past, present or future. Now as a side note; let me just say that, once you've accepted your salvation through Jesus Christ, you can behave any way you like (short of renouncing God), and you won't go to the "bad place".

Let me; however, make this perfectly clear; the New Testament Bible scriptures are there for a reason; not as laws for you to "obey or die", as in the Old Testament; but as instructions on how to live a life that reflects your new righteous nature; the righteous nature freely given by God (to those who accept it), through Jesus Christ, so that you may experience the Kingdom of God right here on earth, as quoted in "The LORD's Prayer": "Thy kingdom come, Thy will be done on earth, as it is in heaven."

Those who accept their salvation in Christ can behave badly, and still go to heaven; however, the choices you make habitually, that are influenced by your fallen human nature (your flesh); rather than your new righteous spirit (the Holy Spirit), will be reflected in your life in one way or another;

resulting in unnecessary grief, set-backs, pain and suffering, and at worse, death (before God's appointed time). So as one preacher puts it: "Who wants to go to heaven by way of hell?!" But, again, that's a whole chapter by itself!

Back to grace. Earlier, I used the term, "entitled to the favour of God". I say this in this way to help those who feel condemned, guilty, or unworthy of God's love and favour. You are entitled to the favour of God not because of what you do, but because of what Jesus did. Sadly, I've met a lot of Christians, or people in general, who feel they're unworthy of the favour of God, and in spite of being really good people (by human standards); the Christians go to God with their begging bowl in their hands like Oliver, talking 'bout, "Please sir, may I have some more.", and the non-Christians, who feel unworthy, don't even bother to approach God, because they think they're supposed to sort themselves out before they can even have the right to ask God for help! I blame this flaw in people's perception of God largely on the religious, self-righteous hypocrites, who see themselves as special in the eyes of God whilst reminding everyone else how "bad" they are; suggesting that God is eager (salivating even) to punish people because of their unrighteous behaviour. This is a religious attack on the good news of the Cross; attempting to turn the gospel of grace back into the very Law of the old covenant that was abolished in Christ!

In Galatians, chapter 3, the great Apostle Paul rebukes the church for this very reason. Please read it!

I've lost count of the times I've heard people say they're too "bad" to go to church. Why do they feel this way? Because of the people who say, "Come to my church, we'll accept you as you are!"; but when they get there, they're made to feel even more condemned, because the grace of the gospel is being preached in the spirit of the old covenant Law! In other words; under the old covenant God made with man, it was: "Do, or else!" However, "Do, or else!" is not the spirit of the gospel of grace! Under this new covenant, it's: "You are forgiven; just believe in your redemption through Jesus Christ." You are further reminded that under the new covenant of grace, you are led by the Holy Spirit; instead of the Old Testament Law, so the choices you make (as you're led by the Holy Spirit) will position you to receive the fulfilment of the purpose of God for your life - which, by the way, is always for your good!

Isaiah 64:6 (KJV) *"But we are all as an unclean thing, and all our righteousnesses are as filthy rags; and we all do fade as a leaf; and our iniquities, like the wind, have taken us away."*

Romans 3:23 (KJV) *"For all have sinned and come short of the glory of God."*

News Flash! Nobody's Righteous! Not of ourselves. This is why grace is so powerful, and so necessary! Only the Holy

Trinity (God, Jesus and The Holy Spirit) is righteous, and we who accept forgiveness through Jesus have righteousness imputed to us (this applies to our spirit only); however, our flesh (our human nature without God) remains corrupt.

This is why I could never find a Christian who behaved like the "perfect righteous person" I thought a Christian was supposed to be. Through Jesus, our spirit is made righteous; but our flesh remains corrupt, hence the Apostle Paul wrote: ***Romans 7:24-25 (KJV) "O wretched man that I am! who shall deliver me from the body of this death? [25] I thank God through Jesus Christ our Lord. So then with the mind I myself serve the law of God; but with the flesh the law of sin."***

Please understand; however, that the grace of God is not a "pass" for your flesh to have dominion in your life. The grace of God is not a pass for you to do, think, and say whatever you like, with impunity. The choices you make that are influenced by your flesh (even as someone in Christ), can make your journey through life very painful. Grace simply gives you access to heaven IN SPITE OF your corrupt nature, because no matter what you do; you will never be perfect, which is why you need Jesus. However, doing, thinking or saying whatever you want, whenever you want, whilst ignoring the leading of the Holy Spirit, is simply taking the grace of God for granted, will make your life difficult on earth, and (dependent upon the motives of your heart) could put you in that situation in heaven, where Jesus says, "I never knew you"! (Matthew 7:21-23)

Romans 8:28 (KJV) "And we know that all things work together for good to them that love God, to them who are the called according to His purpose." The entire New Testament scriptures are for our enlightenment, our instruction, and our correction; but they are not laws! The allowance the Word of God (the scriptures) makes for our stumbling, caused by our corrupt flesh, is that God will even cause our stumbling to work for our good; but only if we cooperate with the leading of the Holy Spirit, and embrace enlightenment, instruction, and correction! ***Psalm 37:23 (KJV) "The steps of a good man are ordered by the Lord, and he delighteth in his way."*** How can God order your steps if you take offense to enlightenment, instruction, and correction?! The spirit of pride is the main thing that causes you to be offended, and that pride, gives shelter to (protects, defends, and makes excuses for) your corrupt nature (your flesh) which then opens the door for the devil to wreak all kinds of havoc in your life!

Grace is available to all of humanity, which means you can accept the salvation made available to you through Christ, without having to qualify for it. Grace continues to cover you as you seek to walk in the character and nature of Christ in spirit and in truth; i.e., with pure motives, whilst at the same time, understanding that you will never achieve total perfection because no matter what you do your corrupted flesh remains with you, so grace is necessary, because without this unearned favour you don't stand a chance, through your own efforts, to enjoy eternal life in heaven with God. ***Colossians 2:10 (KJV) "And ye are complete in him, which is the head of all principality and power."*** The good news is, because of grace; God sees you as complete in Christ.

You should know; however, that grace alone will not get you the "Kingdom of God life" here on earth that God desires for you; as well as, eternal life in heaven. No. Grace by itself (without your cooperation with the Holy Spirit), will not do that. Otherwise, absolutely everyone on the planet would be living a magnificent life, because God's grace is extended to ALL of mankind. So that's not how grace operates. God expects you to cooperate with the Holy Spirit and His Word, in accordance with this new covenant of grace; otherwise, there would be no New Testament scriptures for your enlightenment, instruction and correction! God would not be like, "Here's some grace, now you'll have a great life, so do whatever you want on earth, and I'll see you all in heaven!" No; that's not what grace is for.

Romans 8:7 (KJV) "Because the carnal mind is enmity against God: for it is not subject to the law of God, neither indeed can be." When you (as Paul did) despise your flesh, because it is hostile towards God, and you embrace the chastisement of your flesh; grace will cover the fact that in spite of all the "good" you may do, you are still (compared to God) corrupt, and not worthy (of yourself) to stand righteous before Him.

So grace is not in place to ensure you enjoy a godly and prosperous life, even when you choose to ignore both the leading of the Holy Spirit, and the New Testament scriptures that are given for your enlightenment, instruction, and correction. The fact is, all scriptures are relevant, and have purpose; however, the New Testament scriptures, which of course represent the new covenant God has made with man, through Christ; are written specifically so that you may know how to access the abundant life that grace has made available! You should; therefore, continually correct yourself; that you may maintain alignment with the New Testament scriptures relating to how it is necessary to think, speak, and behave; in order that your flesh doesn't end up having so much influence in your life that the only thing grace is able to do for you, is get you into heaven; because, like I said earlier, who wants to go to heaven by way of hell?! You should always be willing to be enlightened, instructed, and corrected by the Holy Spirit, through the scriptures.

Now having said all of that; there are four things that are not covered by grace. Four things that cannot be absent from your life if you are to enjoy the goodness of God here on earth, and ultimately, experience eternal life in heaven. What are they? Love, gratitude, forgiveness and faith.

Grace does not make the goodness of God, and eternal life in heaven a "done deal", in spite of the unrepentant darkness lurking in your heart. There are people, whom Jesus says He will turn away from entering into heaven; even though they will insist that they were doing great things in His name! (Matthew 7:21-23) I talk about this in greater detail later, in another chapter; but for now, let me just say that grace is not a "Get out of jail free card". Grace; instead, is the lens through which God sees us as we stumble and bumble our way through the journey of life; making mistakes; but striving every day to be led by the Holy Spirit concerning all things. Grace makes allowances for our imperfections; however, does not make allowances for hate, ungratefulness, unwillingness to forgive and unbelief. Those things have to be sorted out in your heart otherwise you risk missing out on God's will for you here on earth, and at worse (if you die without sorting it out) eternal life in heaven itself.

In life, the measure of the "God ordained" abundant life you enjoy (both spiritual and natural) will be determined by the level of consistency in which you walk in love, gratitude, forgiveness, and faith. Now the key word here is, "consistency"; nonetheless, this abundant life cannot (in general) be diminished by your (ever present) sinful nature. I say, "in general" because of what I said earlier; in that the more you yield to your flesh; rather than the Holy Spirit, the less you will see the purpose of God manifesting in your life; however, no matter how much you yield to the Holy Spirit, your sinful nature remains ever present with you, so grace is necessary in any case.

So be encouraged, because of Jesus, if you have accepted His sacrifice; your sinful nature is no longer a factor in determining the measure of favour and blessings you receive from God. God forgave you, and you remain forgiven; however, your human nature is corrupt and will always be corrupt, so God, through grace, has removed your sinful nature from the equation; notwithstanding, you still must allow yourself to be led by the Holy Spirit, and ultimately, the more you can walk in love, gratitude, forgiveness, and faith; the more you will see the power and purpose of God manifested in your life. Now to conclude this thought; apart from the afore mentioned four things which could cause you to miss out on heaven altogether; because of grace, your flesh (your sinful nature) has been relegated to (if you habitually yield to it) causing your life on earth to be turmoiled and troubled, and the worst that could happen (assuming you keep love, gratitude, forgiveness, and faith in your heart), is that you may be all beaten up by life; but you will get to heaven.

So let's examine the four things: The scripture, where the man says "help thou my unbelief" (Mark 9:24 KJV), is not to be interpreted as it not being a big deal if you don't believe; suggesting that (if you ask Him) God will give you faith. No! Faith, unconditional love, gratitude and forgiveness is a big deal as far as God is concerned, and is completely and totally down to you. The measure by which you consistently walk in these four things will most definitely determine the measure of abundant life you enjoy on earth! Sadly, what the man was saying in Mark 9:24 was, there are times when he doesn't believe. That is not good. Why? Because if you have unbelief, ungratefulness, unforgivness or hate in your heart, they will most certainly disrupt the connection between you and God; preventing His purpose from being fulfilled in that particular situation, or even in future situations, depending upon how long you struggle in any of these four areas. Why? Because your flesh will make sure it does!

Your flesh (your fallen nature) is hostile towards God, and opposes the spiritual and natural prosperity that is available to you when you surrender to the leading of the Holy Spirit. Don't get me wrong, you can acquire stuff through the workings of your flesh; however, your flesh is incapable of nurturing the purpose of God for your life; therefore, your flesh by default, keeps you prisoner to the trappings of a fallen world which (sadly) includes the inability to comprehend spiritual things.

So it is imperative that you are not only consistent in faith, but in love, gratitude and forgiveness. Just a note here: Do not mistake wealth and notoriety as a barometer for success, for if it is acquired through the workings of your flesh and not the leading of the Holy Spirit; then it will profit you nothing in the end, when your brief existence (compared to eternity) on this earth has expired.

But, let me be clear, admitting to sometimes saying or doing things that are inconsistent with love, gratitude, forgiveness and faith does not mean you're incapable of expressing love, gratitude, forgiveness and faith; it makes you human, with all our flaws. However, it's better to admit that sometimes you will say, or do things that comes from your flesh, and for you to be teachable and humble enough to be corrected, than to assume that just because you "think" you're righteous, you can't possibly say or do something to the contrary. It's better (like the Apostle Paul) to say, I am a wretch (referring to his flesh), but I thank God for the redemptive power of Jesus Christ in whom I live, move and have my being. It is better for you to acknowledge that the only righteousness in you is of God, and strive to be totally consumed by His righteousness, that it may increase, and your flesh decrease.

When we humble ourselves the way Paul did, and willingly accept how far from the beauty and holiness of God our flesh really is, we (as did Paul) will not have a problem recognising and rejecting the things we say, think and do that are inconsistent with the character and nature of Jesus Christ, who is righteousness personified. We should be so delivered from pride, and the condemnation of our flesh, and (like Paul) so repulsed by our fallen nature, that we dare not make excuses for it! The scripture (James 5:16 KJV) says we should confess our faults to one another, which means we should be honest with each other (and with ourselves) regarding our flaws. YOU ARE NOT CONDEMNED! So please give pride a kick in the butt, and stop denying your shortcomings; instead acknowledge and REJECT them! If the great Apostle Paul had the humility to do it, so can you!

Still on the subject of the four things not covered by grace, "What?! Is he still banging on about that?!" Yes I am, so bare with me! God says (1Cor 13:1-3), if you do every single thing the scriptures instruct you to do, but love is absent in you; then it will profit you nothing! It cost Jesus everything to love you, so love is something you should not be struggling with. There is no grace to cover the absence of love for one another! God requires us to love one another, and it should not be conditional. It should not be based on how we're feeling in the moment or even how we're treated - "I love you; but only if you...". That's not love; but that's another whole chapter all by itself!

Now what about gratitude? Will grace cover us even if we're ungrateful? ***1 Thessalonians 5:18 (KJV) "In everything give thanks: for this is the will of God in Christ Jesus concerning you."*** Many people unconsciously give God thanks for just the "big stuff"; but "everything" means "everything"! Do not let an ungrateful heart deprive you of the blessings of God. Don't get me wrong, God is even kind to the unthankful and to the evil (Luke 6:35); however, this is so that they might be led by His goodness, to change their ways (repent), and accept the salvation made available to them, for it is not God's will that they perish (2 Peter 3:9). It's also for our example, because we are instructed to love our enemies; but when you have experienced the goodness and the mercy of God over and over again, yet you still remain ungrateful; then you are tempting Christ, which is never a good thing and will most likely lead to you losing that which you already have. Why? Because as with all things spiritual, understanding is key. If you lack the understanding of why it's necessary and important to be grateful then you won't be consistent in gratefulness or at worst, be flat out ungrateful period, which will lead to a life of misery! Will it stop you from going to heaven? That depends on whether your ungratefulness evolves into resentment and hate towards God, which unfortunately tends to happen to people who lack understanding about being grateful, or lack understanding concerning spiritual things in general.

What about being unforgiving? **Mark 11:26 (KJV). "But if ye do not forgive, neither will your Father which is in heaven forgive your trespasses."** You can't get into heaven without God's forgiveness, so that's pretty straightforward!

Finally, faith. You need faith to believe in your salvation so that's covered right there; no faith in salvation, no heaven. In cases where you believe in your salvation; however, you lack in faith when it comes to other things; then grace will keep you; but you will be living well beneath your privilege; living off scraps by God's standards, and not the full provisions He has made available to you through Jesus. If you only have faith for your salvation, and absolutely nothing else; then you'll get to heaven; but on earth you'll be broke, busted and disgusted!

So, in conclusion, and to summarise: God will not love on your behalf, in other words, you cannot be walking in hate towards someone, and expect the grace of God to cover for you. If you're hateful, and you don't change and surrender to love, and you die in that hate; your spirit will perish in hell. Likewise, God will not give you gratitude, it's up to you to be grateful. The thing about gratitude is, if you are an ungrateful person; ungratefulness opens the door to bitterness, which opens the door to resentment which, if unresolved, leads to hate, and you're back on that dusty road to hell. God will not make you forgive someone; that's your job. Whatever you're struggling to forgive will never be greater than what Jesus went through to forgive you so that you can spend eternity in heaven; hence God says, forgive; otherwise, you will not be forgiven, which means no heaven. Finally, faith. Even if you lack faith for everything provided for you through grace; you must have faith for your salvation, or it's the "bad place" again!

By the way, you didn't think you'd get through this whole book without me mentioning hell did you? Hell is real, just as real as heaven. There's no point acknowledging the existence of heaven, without acknowledging the existence of hell. The thing is, it is not God's will or desire for anyone to perish in hell (2 Peter 3:9); neither is it God's desire that we come to Him because we're afraid of going to hell! The goodness, mercy, grace and unconditional love of God is more than enough reason for us to seek Him out. The devil is a former angel (not even a high ranking one), created by God Himself, so coming to God for fear of going to hell; gives Satan too much credit, and is an insult to the goodness, love and majesty of God.

Before I understood the difference between the old covenant God established with humanity, and the new covenant; I used to read the Bible with much trepidation, because all I could see was condemnation! All I could see was that no matter what I did; I was likely going to hell - especially according to the Old Testament scriptures because I was breaking more laws than Bonnie and Clyde! Now that I understand the character and nature of Jesus, who says, "He that has seen me, has seen the Father". Now that I understand the true meaning of the gospel, which is a gospel of grace; I can now read and use all scriptures without feeling condemned, because I now put them into proper context, especially Old Testament scriptures relating to the Law! So we should not just simply ignore or disregard the Old Testament scriptures because: **2 Timothy 3:16-17 (KJV) [16] "ALL scripture is given by inspiration of God, and is profitable for doctrine, for reproof, for correction, for instruction in righteousness: [17] That the man of God may be perfect, throughly furnished unto all good works."** The thing is, some church folk mix the old covenant with the new covenant (without distinguishing the difference), so that they might rule over people; keeping them in bondage, when the grace of the gospel is meant to set them free.

So no matter what you do, you will never be able to "earn" grace, you don't deserve it of yourself; it is the free gift from God that allows you to (in spite of yourself) enjoy His goodness in this life, and ultimately, entrance into the Kingdom of heaven. I can imagine God in heaven; shaking His head saying, "These folks I've made; they are a mess...I'm just gonna have to forgive them."

Don't try to impress me with how many scriptures you know; impress me with the good you've accomplished with the scriptures you know.

CHAPTER 4

How Do You Plead? Guilty or Not Guilty?

Faith is a powerful thing; however, you should know that guilt is also powerful. In fact guilt is so powerful, that it can even block, or cancel out faith! Gladly, Jesus freed us from guilt and shame, so that the way could be cleared for faith to operate in our lives.

Genesis 15:6 (KJV) "And he believed in the Lord; and he counted it to him for righteousness." Romans 4:3 (KJV) "For what saith the scripture? Abraham believed God, and it was counted unto him for righteousness." Today, God sees us as righteous when we believe that Jesus was sacrificed, and that He rose again on our behalf. The above two scriptures speak of Abraham believing God, and in return, God credits Abraham's faith to him as righteousness. This of course was long before the new covenant of grace that we currently live under, which makes it all the more incredible that such was Abraham's faith in God, that in spite of all his imperfections; guilt and condemnation was powerless against Abraham's faith! Wow!!

All the guilt of humanity was removed when Jesus died and rose again. "If Jesus freed me from guilt then why do I still feel guilty?" I hear you say? Well firstly, let's examine how Jesus removed our guilt:

When Adam and Eve committed the first act of disobedience, causing them to know both good and evil; the Bible says they, for the first time, became aware of their nakedness, and were ashamed (Genesis 3:7). This was the origin of guilt! So once again, ole Adam and Eve wrecked things for the rest of us! So how did knowing both good and evil cause Adam and Eve to realise they were naked? As I said in the previous chapter; although we're made in the image of God, making us gods ourselves (Psalm 82:6 and John 10:34); we do not possess the capacity (like God) to know evil and not be influenced or affected by it, therefore the inherent corrupted nature of evil caused Adam and Eve to see each other through the eyes of sexual lust and desire; causing them to feel guilty and shameful, so they covered their naughty bits.

For generations, from the days after the first act of disobedience by Adam and Eve, to the time of Noah and the flood, and for generations afterwards; humanity had no measurable means by which to determine how far we'd drifted from the former glorified state-of-being we enjoyed before that first act of disobedience (which from here on I'll refer to as "the fall"). After the fall, the Bible (Genesis 3:16-19) speaks of the punishment decreed by God upon humanity, which in short was: (1) Losing our relationship with animals, where we went from (literally) being able to have conversations with them; to some animals becoming a threat to our lives and wellbeing, and others becoming a source of sustenance and clothing. (2) Having to work hard to earn a living, where we once just "chilled" in the land, and God provided all that we needed. (3) Being cast out from the special land God created for us; the Garden of Eden (where we were "chillin"), which contained the tree of life from which, if we ate, we'd live forever. In short, this was the punishment that came upon humanity because of that first act of disobedience; however, all the selfishness and debauchery that came afterwards, and continues to this day; that's on us!

I'm still explaining how Jesus removed humanity's guilt, so stay with me.

For generations after the fall, there were no written laws from God, or any other measurable means by which we could be made aware of how far we'd drifted from the state of glory and perfection that once defined us. There was nothing we could refer to which held us accountable for our corrupted state. So life was pretty much a "free for all"! Then, God decides to wipe all of humanity from the earth, and start over again (Genesis chapter 6). Fortunately, God found one good man (Noah) and his family who, in spite of the hardships decreed upon humanity; remained good and honourable, and found favour in the sight of God.

When Noah warned the people of that time that he was instructed by God to build a boat because God was going to destroy all humankind, the people scoffed at Noah and his family, and went about their wicked ways; however, when the deluge started, they all stormed the boat Noah built, begging to be let in; but Noah was like, "Nope!"

Many generations after the flood, God singled out Moses, and to him was given the Law; the written Commandments of God (Exodus chapter 24), which became the means by which humanity would now know the totality of its invariable fallen nature.

The Law of God, as defined under the old covenant, is humanity's mirror, and when we look into it; it reflects our guilt. Why does the law make us guilty? Because it is impossible for us to fulfil it! And how about this: ***James 2:10 (Amp) "For whosoever keeps the Law as a whole but stumbles and offends in one single instance has become guilty of breaking all of it."*** Wow! Okay, so the Law of God makes us guilty because it is impossible for us to fulfill it. Fortunately for us, Jesus fulfilled the Law! ***Matthew 5:17 (KJV) "Think not that I am come to destroy the law, or the prophets: I am not come to destroy, but to fulfil."*** When Jesus sacrificed himself on our behalf (taking the blame for our guilt), we (those who believe) became free from guilt, and not just guilt, but the condemnation and shame associated with it.

So why do you still feel guilty even after accepting the forgiveness of God through Jesus Christ? It's because although your spirit has been renewed; your flesh (your fallen nature) remains intact, and forever attempting to influence your thoughts, words and actions. "Sinful" can be defined as the nature of fallen humanity, whilst "sin" can be defined as the byproduct of fallen humanity. If you believe in your salvation through Jesus, your sinful nature remains ever present; however, the byproduct of your sinful nature ("sin") no longer has dominion over you. ***Romans 6:14 (KJV) "For sin shall not have dominion over you: for ye are not under the law, but under grace."*** In other words; the affects as well as the consequences of sin has been removed from you. Nonetheless, even though sin no longer has dominion over you, the sinful nature remains with you; coexisting alongside your new righteous nature, which means you will sometimes be influenced by your sinful nature, which includes feeling guilty.

So it's incumbent upon you to first recognise the difference between your fallen nature and your righteous nature in Christ. You must be able to identify your thoughts, words and actions that are inconsistent with the character and nature of Christ, and reject them. Asking yourself, "What would Jesus do?" is pointless if you don't know Him, so it's important that you study the words Jesus has spoken, and the scriptures relating to Him that reveals His heart towards humanity. You also must become deeply acquainted with the Holy Spirit, whom God sent to us in Jesus' name (John 14:26). So meditation on the Word of God and prayer is essential.

Still on the topic of why you still feel guilty even though you believe in your forgiveness through Christ: Well, it doesn't help that many people (including Christians) heap judgement and condemnation on you; notwithstanding, our sinful nature does tend to stick to us like smoke residue. Have you ever barbecued, or been to a barbecue, and the smell of the smoke gets on your clothes, your skin, and in your hair? Well, just because you smell like barbecue, doesn't mean you have to be served up with the chicken, pork ribs, beef ribs, brisket, burgers, steak, hotdogs, sausages, corn-on-the-cob... Uh-oh, I made myself hungry; give me a moment...

Now, where was I?! Oh yeah. What I'm trying to say is that you are not barbecue, you just smell like it! When you accept Christ in your life, you become washed clean through the sacrifice of His blood. Your spirit becomes one with Jesus, and you become a new creation. ***2 Corinthians 5:17 (KJV) "Therefore if any man be in Christ, he is a new creature: old things are passed away; behold, all things are become new."*** Nonetheless, your old (sinful) nature sticks to you like smoke residue, and every now and then, that "smell" (your old sinful nature) influences how you think, feel, speak and behave; however, what you must know is that just because you might "smell" like a sinner, you are no longer a sinner! You are a new creation! You are in Christ!!

Psalm 103:12 (KJV) "As far as the east is from the west, so far hath he removed our transgressions from us." God no longer sees your sinful nature, you are no longer guilty before God, therefore you should no longer give guilt authority in your life by feeling guilty! ***2 Corinthians 5:21 (KJV) "For he hath made him to be sin for us, who knew no sin; that we might be made the righteousness of God in him."*** Your spirit has been made righteous; just like Jesus!

Allow yourself to be led by the Holy Spirit so that you may yield to your new righteous nature in Christ; rather than your old sinful nature. The more you do this; the less you will yield to your old nature, and before you know it; you will find it easy to flow in the spirit of righteousness in your thinking, your speaking, and in your actions, and you will walk in the power of the Holy Spirit; causing guilt, condemnation, and shame to slide off you like butter off a hot knife!

We love in part only, for love is a journey of revelation, sacrifice, and development which we never fully complete.

CHAPTER 5

I Agree With That

What does it mean to be in spiritual agreement? Is spiritual agreement important? Absolutely! You are in spiritual agreement when two or more people who are in Christ, and are led of the Holy Spirit, are able to see, hear and feel the same spiritual things, as it pertains to the issues and circumstances of life. In other words, these two or more people will be in harmony because they share the same spiritual understandings. They may have different levels of understanding as in, one may have more spiritual understanding about things than the other, which is okay. However, the more spiritual understanding you have in common, the less of a stumbling block you'll be to one another, and the more effective your prayers will be; particularly when it comes to speaking into existence that which God has purposed for you as a couple or a group.

Did I say, "Speak into existence?" Yes I did! Spiritual agreement allows you to pray with precision, focus and power! Also, instead of treading on each other's "toes" because of not being on the same page; spiritual agreement gives you the ability to flow together through the challenges of life with ease, and with purpose, as you (together) pursue the will of God for your lives. I've got to tell you (because it's absolutely crucial that you know) that loving one another just isn't enough! You've gotta know, believe, and understand some stuff...together!!

Have you ever heard anyone use term "agree to disagree"? Of all the completely ridiculous things I've ever heard; that statement ranks supreme on my list! Sadly this saying has crept into relationships; hindering couples (and groups) from maximising their potential, and causing them to fall short of what they could achieve if they were in agreement concerning all things. Now when I say, "All things", I'm not referring to liking the same colours or the same toppings on your pizza, which is fine if that's the case; however, what I'm referring to is all things spiritual.

Spiritual agreement will even affect the way you behave towards one another. You know you're in agreement when you do, or desire to do things for each other, just because you like the idea of doing it; instead of doing it purely out of duty, or because you're expected to behave a certain way. When you're in agreement, you like the way it makes you feel when you see the person (or people) you're in agreement with being blessed; especially if it's of your doing; however, you expect nothing in return because their pleasure is reward enough.

Let's talk about faith and how it relates to agreement, because they are two separate things; however, they both are a necessity in our Christian lives, and (ideally) should be used together where more than one person is involved.

Matthew 18:19 (KJV) "Again I say unto you, That if two of you shall agree on earth as touching any thing that they shall ask, it shall be done for them of my Father which is in heaven." This is the Word of God, and not speculation, or assumption.

Jesus is emphasising "agreement" here, and not faith; but of course faith is implied in the "asking". When more than one person is involved, the "asking" is by faith, but the result comes by being in agreement! Our challenge is understanding what it really means to be in agreement; I mean God's definition of agreement, so let's get into this...

I remember a pastor's testimony, about the doctor saying that his son would not likely survive the night in hospital, after experiencing massive convulsions, due to serious health complications. The pastor said his wife went from the hospital room crying; but he remained, and he declared that his son would not die! The pastor said he assigned four angels (one for each corner of his son's bed); then left the hospital with his wife. Of course, their son lived.

So, what happened here? Did the wife have faith in that moment? No. Did the pastor? Yes. So even though only one of them had faith; faith was indeed activated. Bam!

Now, did the wife want her son to live? Absolutely! Did the pastor want his son to live? Absolutely! So then we have agreement, right? Wrong! Just because they wanted the same thing did not put them in agreement! What put them in agreement was the fact that they (for starters) were both "in Christ"; but also, they both possessed spiritual understanding about God's power, and ability to save their son! The pastor simply had the faith to speak it! One person (the pastor) had faith; however, they both were in agreement via their spiritual understanding regarding God's power. That was enough to achieve the desired result. Double Bam!! Agreement and faith are two separate things, and it is imperative that we know the difference, as well as (in cases where two or more people are involved) the necessity for both.

Our human existence or presence here, in the natural; is but the thin, top layer of who we are in totality. We (all humans) are in essence spiritual beings. In the natural, we can speak and perform in ways to project a certain image, or to portray a particular attitude; however, the greater part of us is our spirit, in which lies our true nature, and is where our true motives exists and are seen by God. Jesus (using a false prophet as an example) said, "I never knew you. Depart from me, you that work iniquity!" Jesus said this to someone who professed he'd been prophesying, casting out devils and doing many wonderful works! All in the name of Jesus! So why did Jesus reject this person?! Because God, Jesus, the Holy Spirit sees the WHOLE of our existence (body, mind and spirit) and knew that this person's motives were not pure; in other words, this person was not doing the will of God. (Mat 7:15-23)

We can say or do something in the natural; however within our spirit (or the spiritual realm) lies our true nature, and our true motives, which is possible to be hidden from some people; but not from God. I say, "Some people", because the Word of God tells us that we are known by our fruit (Matthew 7:15-20), and some people have the ability to discern the true motives, or source behind a person's words or actions. What are your words and actions producing in the people around you? What effect are you having on people? Can the "good" you're doing be quantified by the Word of God? What "fruit" is being produced by your children, or by your spouse because of your words or actions?

As relating to being in spiritual agreement with your spouse, partner, or collective; the evidence of agreement is in the fruit, or lack thereof. For example, God had to intervene regarding the Tower of Babel because God said, "The people are one", (Genesis 11:6). "One" meaning the people were in agreement, so if God didn't cause confusion amongst them, by giving them different languages so that they could no longer understand each other; God said (Genesis 11:6), "nothing they have imagined they can do will be impossible for them." Faith in God is not mentioned here at all, because humans don't need God to get stuff done; all we need is agreement! Regarding the Tower of Babel, the people were in agreement because they were all of one mind, regarding the building of the tower; in other words, they all had the same desire to see the tower constructed, and they all possessed the same determination to complete it. I also like to use evil people like Hitler as another example, just to stress this point even further; because Hitler (and all the evil people in agreement with him) nearly conquered the world! Faith in God as well as (and specifically) spiritual agreement; however, is necessary for the believer, for God says, it profits us nothing to gain the world; but lose our souls (Mark 8:36). Hitler died, and his spirit is spending eternity in hell, along with anyone else who died whilst being in agreement with him, so even though the power of agreement made it possible for them to nearly conquer the world; it profited them nothing in the end which; by the way, happens to be eternal. The subject of agreement is big; but absolutely necessary to address, and is not impossible to understand.

So how do you (the Christian) come into spiritual agreement with other Christians? By seeing one another, as well as the challenges you face, through the eyes of the Holy Spirit who; by the way, happens to reside in you. Your question should be, "How does God see me?" Your response should be, "That's how I want to see myself." Regarding whomever you're in relationship with, your question should be, "How does God see them?" Your response should be, "That's how I want to see them." Your question should be, "How does God see the challenges we face together?" Your response should be, "That's how I want to see the challenges we face together." In so doing, where two or more are involved; it will be impossible for your flesh to oppose the will of God for you both (or all) in any given situation. Do you see the power and the victory in this?!

Ephesians 3:20 "Now unto him that is able to do exceeding abundantly above all that we ask or think, according to the power that works in us..." The key words here are, "according to the power that works in us." What has God purposed for your life? For some of us, "To whom much is given, much is required." applies; therefore (for some of us), God requires both faith and spiritual agreement to be operational in all parties concerned. Referencing Deuteronomy 32:30: With God on our side, one can put a thousand to flight, and two, ten thousand! What are the possibilities when all parties concerned possess both faith in God and spiritual agreement?!

For the purpose of God to be fulfilled in your lives (where two or more are concerned), God requires you to be in spiritual agreement; however, God will not force His purpose upon you. Neither will He force upon you the provisions relating to His purpose. God's grace keeps you and provides for you as you journey towards your ultimate purpose; however, the provisions provided by God's grace, the "streams in the desert", or the "crumbs from the Master's table", were never meant to be your final destination! God means for you to leave the desert! God means for you to sit at the table! For some of us; however (where two or more are involved), where "to whom much has been given; therefore, much is required" applies; faith is not enough to leave the desert, or to sit at the table; we must have faith, and we must be in spiritual agreement!

The "two of you" Jesus is referring to in Mat 18:19 are God's people, not non-believers, hence Jesus says, "...it will be done for them by my Father in heaven." God was not responsible for the building of the Tower of Babel. God was not the spiritual force behind Hitler's campaign. The people "agreeing" to accomplish these things, was enough to get results. Humanity can accomplish stuff simply by agreeing to do it; but we must be in spiritual agreement (in Christ) for God's purpose to be accomplished

I Agree With That

in the Christian. Can a Christian get stuff done without God? Yes, of course, Christians are humans, made in the image of God. So even Christians can get stuff done through the flesh, through sheer one mindedness and determination; however, it will not be of God; i.e., it will not be God's will, or in alignment with His purpose. It's spiritual agreement with one another through Christ; that's what gets God involved with what we agree to (or do) in the natural, here on earth. This is why it's so important to understand what spiritual agreement really means!

Shall we go deeper? That is, assuming you're still with me! If you are; then God bless you, because this is a lot to take in; but I hope you're getting it...

The evidence of agreement in a Godly relationship isn't in saying you want the same things, but in the edification of one another by your thoughts, words and actions. Why is this true? It's true because the believer's spirit is ALREADY in agreement with the Holy Spirit! That was sorted when you accepted your salvation, and spiritually became the righteousness of God. Notwithstanding, it is a constant battle with the flesh to walk in spiritual agreement through Christ, because although we are indeed the righteousness of God, and a new creation in Christ; our flesh opposes this state of existence - constantly! This is why the apostle Paul (of all people!) said in Romans 7:14-23 that he was doing stuff he didn't want to do! Paul's flesh was in opposition with his righteous spirit even though his righteous spirit was in agreement with the Holy Spirit! That aside; when two or more people come into agreement with the Holy Spirit, they become in agreement with each other, by default!

Think of the Holy Spirit as electricity, and yourself as copper wire. When electricity goes through copper wire, the electricity is the same before it gets inside the wire, and it remains the same whilst in the wire. The potency of the electricity may change, however it's properties, the molecular structure that defines it as electricity does not, it remains constant, and it never changes. Our spirit is in agreement with the Holy Spirit; therefore, God's loving attitude towards us (like electricity through metal) should become our attitude towards each other, and the same goes for God's desires for us, they should become our desires for each other; but, check this out; this is the problem, and this is huge:

Our "flesh" (our fallen nature) behaves like a non-conductive material, like wood or rubber for instance, and like wood or rubber; it blocks electricity. Our flesh blocks the influence of the Holy Spirit in us, and through us. This blockage is what we see in action when (because of the influence of our flesh) our thoughts, attitude, or behaviour towards one another is not edifying; instead, destructive. Our thoughts, words and actions become inconsistent with Christians who are actually in spiritual agreement with each other by way of Christ! Can you see it!? The-devil-is-a-liar-and-so-is-our-flesh!!

Hosea 4:6 (KJV) "My people are destroyed for lack of knowledge..." So what do we need to know here; what do we need to understand? We need to understand that those who are in Christ, have been made the righteousness of God; therefore, we (by default) are in agreement with each other! John 14:20 says Jesus is in The Father, we are in Jesus, and Jesus is in us. That makes us all in spiritual agreement! It's impossible for this not to be the case! Spiritual agreement is not a feeling; it's a state of being! When we allow ourselves to be influenced by our flesh, we are hindered from seeing ourselves as "in agreement" with one another as we truly are; therefore, our thoughts, words, and our behaviour towards one another becomes destructive, and will most definitely hinder the will and the purpose of God for our lives.

Matthew 6:33 (KJV) "But seek ye first the kingdom of God, and His righteousness; and all these things shall be added unto you." God will not send blessings in response to the actions of our flesh. Jesus makes this clear with His instructions to us to avoid seeking stuff the way unbelievers do; instead, seek the Kingdom of God and His righteousness. Don't get me wrong, like I already said; you can make things happen for yourself without God; however, it won't be "of" God.

Your salvation is the product of the grace of God; however, grace alone will not give you the abundant life God desires for you; spiritual knowledge with understanding will do that. The hindering, or sabotaging behaviour of your flesh can take many forms in a relationship; but it will be unique to that relationship, with the intent to disrupt or to defeat the plans and the purpose of God for you. Please remember, no matter how "nice" you think you are, your flesh remains hostile towards God, and (by default) is determined to destroy the plans of God for you, and in extreme cases, blasphemy for instance (Matthew 12:31-32), will even nullify your salvation.

Please remember that agreement means being connected to, or being in harmony with; whereby, the thoughts and actions of the one is consistent (in harmony) with the thoughts and actions of the other(s). Acts 2:1 refers to agreement as being, "with one accord".

So where two or more are involved; the more you resist your flesh so that the Holy Spirit may work through you in every thought, word, or action, and in every situation and circumstance, and the more spiritual understanding you have in common with one another; the more you will experience the manifestation of the purpose and provision of God in your lives.

For those who are in Christ; the level, or the amount of agreement in their Christian relationships, is determined by the extent of their shared knowledge and understanding of spiritual truths, coupled with the extent of their shared ability to live by it. Just understanding this statement alone, and pursuing it, will give you all the ammunition you require to walk in total and complete spiritual agreement with one another.

Behaving contrary to righteousness is not a problem of itself; the "why" we do it is the problem.

CHAPTER 6

I Just Wanna Be Myself!

Generally, people don't like thinking about their flaws because it makes them feel guilty, so people avoid acknowledging them; however, for me, there's nothing more liberating than being fully aware of my fallen nature. I'm fully aware of my flaws, my "dark" side so to speak, so for me, my life is like walking through a minefield; but I'm able to stay on the right path because I know exactly where all the mines are! Ha! Totally, and completely liberating!

A person who is in Christ (born again), does not commit sins. What?! Yes, you heard me! ***1 John 3:2 (KJV) "Beloved, now are we the sons of God, and it doth not yet appear what we shall be: but we know that, when he shall appear, we shall be like him; for we shall see him as he is."***

1 John 3:9 (KJV) "Whosoever is born of God doth not commit sin; for His seed remaineth in him: and he cannot sin, because he is born of God." Also, please read Romans, chapter 6! The flesh influenced behaviour of a person who is in Christ, is not seen as sin by God, for God (because of Jesus' sacrifice) only sees the righteousness of Christ. ***2 Corinthians 5:21 (KJV) "For he hath made him to be sin for us, who knew no sin; that we might be made the righteousness of God in him."*** Remember, if you are in Christ; then you are a new creation (2 Corinthians 5:17); however, depending on your level of obedience to the leading of the Holy Spirit, your flesh motivated behaviour can cause havoc in your life, and at worst, make your Christian experience painful and wrought with troubles. You'll get to heaven, but it could be a very painful and weary journey.

In Romans, chapter 6, the Apostle Paul reminds us that those who are in Christ, died to sin with Christ. So Paul explains that we shouldn't continue to behave as if are yet still sinners! Actually, sin applies to those who are not in Christ; who have not accepted the free gift of salvation, redemption, atonement and who are; therefore, still judged by the Law! James chapter 4 speaks about sinners; those who are not in Christ; therefore, are still judged by the old covenant Law; it finishes with this: **James 4:17 (KJV) "Therefore to him that knoweth to do good, and doeth it not, to him it is sin."** When you read the scriptures with understanding, through the guidance of the Holy Spirit; you'll find that there are no contradictions in the Word of God.

The more you feel bad about yourself, the more you're likely to behave badly; i.e., contrary to righteousness. You feel bad, so you behave contrary to righteousness (or sin, for the non-believer) to make yourself feel good, and before you know it; you're stuck in a loop!

So why does committing acts of sin make people feel good? It's simple really. We connect with, or identify with sin and this fallen world, through our flesh (our fallen/corrupt human nature), so doing sinful things appeases our flesh and makes us feel good. For example: if you're addicted to a drug or alcohol; your body needs those substances to make you feel good, and without it, you feel bad. Sinful behaviour is the "drug", or "alcohol" for the flesh (our fallen nature). Sinful behaviour makes the flesh feel good; but only the flesh! We are fallen beings, living in a fallen world; therefore, we are constantly bombarded by things designed to appeal to our flesh; instead of our righteous spirit. So (in this fallen world) it's easier to appease our flesh than it is to defer to our righteous nature and be led by the Holy Spirit. Being a fallen creation in a fallen world; it is easier to do bad than it is to do good. This is why Jesus says, **Matthew 7:13-14 (Amp) [13]** *"Enter through the narrow gate; for wide is the gate and spacious and broad is the way that leads away to destruction, and many are those who are entering through it. [14] But the gate is narrow (contracted by pressure) and the way is straitened and compressed that leads away to life, and few are those who find it."*

As a Christian; behaving in alignment with our new righteous nature is challenging in a fallen world that, by default, appeals to our flesh. The thing is, just because something feels good doesn't mean it's good for us. This is not meant to discourage you, absolutely not; in fact, to the contrary, because knowledge and understanding is power! When you know better, when you understand; you have the opportunity to do, and to be better!

Here are a few questions:

1. What is the purpose of the New Testament scriptures relating to our behaviour?
2. What benefit is there in having them operating in our lives?
3. Are the New Testament scriptures laws?

4. Are we punished if we don't obey the New Testament scriptures?

Here are some answers:

God created His divine Law (in the Old Testament) to expose the flaws and wickedness of humanity, and to accentuate the degree to which humanity has fallen from the state of uncorrupted perfection we once were when God placed us in a garden He created, which was eastward in Eden (Genesis 2:8). The reason the Old Testament Law exposes our true nature, is because to fulfill it, we'd have to be absolutely perfect! The way we were before the "fall"! You could say it's God's way of saying, "Uh, hey humans, y'all ain't all that!" The Old Testament Law represents God's old covenant with humanity, and was simply meant to be a "Schoolmaster" (Galatians 3:24) to keep us in favour with God until the completion of the new covenant, which is the forgiveness of all sin, for all time, through Jesus' sacrifice on the cross; God's new covenant of grace.

Romans 8:3 (Amp) "For God has done what the Law could not do, its power being weakened by the flesh, the entire nature of man without the Holy Spirit. Sending His own Son in the guise of sinful flesh and as an offering for sin, God condemned sin in the flesh subdued, overcame, deprived it of its power over all who accept that sacrifice." The entire nature of man without the Holy Spirit is hostile towards God and condemned by the Law of God. If you have not accepted the salvation which is offered through Jesus Christ, by God's divine grace; then you are still subject to the judgment, condemnation and punishment of the old covenant Laws.

Colossians 2:13 (KJV) "And you, being dead in your sins and the uncircumcision of your flesh, hath he quickened together with him, having forgiven you all trespasses." Jesus Christ is sinless, and we (those who've accepted the free gift of salvation) are in Christ; therefore, sin no longer has dominion over us. Now if sin no longer has dominion over us (Romans 6:14); then neither can the consequences of sin affect us, for our old nature has been stripped of its power over us, and we have become the righteousness of God through Jesus. We; therefore, cannot be both in Christ, at one with Him, and yet still be subject to the consequences of sin at the same time! Now if you don't understand this, if you don't believe this (even though you've accepted your salvation, and are in Christ); life will beat up on you just as if you hadn't been delivered from the dominion of sin at all!

Say for example, someone opens an account in your name, deposits millions of dollars in it, tells you about it; but you don't believe it. In fact, you don't even check with the bank! So what happens? You walk around behaving like you're broke, when actually, you aren't, and you could be living large and taking charge!

For many Christians, they allow their behaviour to (in their mind and in their heart) disqualify them from the blessings of God! If you're a Christian, and you're still being beaten up by life, or you're not seeing that "abundant" life you were promised in Christ; I've come to tell you that you cannot "behave" your way out of it! You simply have to believe that sin no longer has dominion over you, and your behaviour will follow! You will realise that there is nothing you can do or not do to earn the grace of God, so you just be yourself (in Christ), and allow the grace of God do what it's meant to do, which is bless you undeservingly! It's not what you do that sets you free, it's what you know! It's what JESUS did that sets you free!

If you truly believe and understand what it means to be dead to sin, if you truly believe and understand what it means for sin to no longer have dominion over you; then that would be reflected in your life by the way you behave, and you will be experiencing the goodness and blessings of God, in spite of still being the flawed human that we all are.

Romans 3:10 (KJV) "As it is written, There is none righteous, no, not one." Romans 3:23-24 (Amp) [23] "Since all have sinned and are falling short of the honor and glory which God bestows and receives. [24] All are justified and made upright and in right standing with God, freely and gratuitously by His grace (His unmerited favor and mercy), through the redemption which is provided in Christ Jesus." A person who knows that Jesus loves them in spite of their imperfections, a person who knows that God loves them even though they deserve death; is a person who's heart doesn't condemn them, a person who is humble before God, and a person whom God can trust to be a good ambassador for the Kingdom of God, under His new covenant of grace.

Romans 7:15 (KJV) *"For that which I do I allow not: for what I would, that do I not; but what I hate, that do I."* Uh, thanks Paul. Now in plain english; what the great Apostle Paul is saying, is that he's baffled because he's doing sinful stuff that he doesn't want to do! In Galatians 5:21, we read that people who do sinful things shall not inherit the Kingdom of God, so does this mean that Paul is in hell? God forbid! Paul further explains in Romans 7:20 (Amp) that it's not actually him that's doing it, but sin in him: *"Now if I do what I do not desire to do, it is no longer I doing it [it is not myself that acts], but the sin [principle] which dwells within me [fixed and operating in my soul].* In Romans 7:25 Paul says, ..."*with the mind I myself serve the law of God, but with the flesh the law of sin."* In Galatians 5:18 (Amp) Paul says, *"But if you are guided (led) by the [Holy] Spirit, you are not subject to the Law"* which of course means; neither can we (who are in Christ) be condemned by the Law!

So what must we understand from all this? We must understand that those of us who believe in the salvation that is available to us through Jesus Christ, have received grace (unmerited and unearned favour); a gift from God! It means that, in spite of our sinful nature remaining ever present and active within us; we (because of our faith in Jesus Christ) are seen as righteous in the eyes of God; nonetheless, we must remember what the Word of God says to us in Galatians 5:13 (Amp) *"For you, brethren, were indeed called to freedom; only do not let your freedom be an incentive to your flesh and an opportunity or excuse for selfishness, but through love you should serve one another."* And what the Word of God says in 1 Corinthians 6:12 (Amp) *"Everything is permissible (allowable and lawful) for me; but not all things are helpful (good for me to do, expedient and profitable when considered with other things). Everything is lawful for me, but I will not become the slave of anything or be brought under its power."* This is repeated here: *1 Corinthians 10:23 (Amplified) "All things are legitimate permissible--and we are free to do anything we please, but not all things are helpful (expedient, profitable, and wholesome). All things are legitimate, but not all things are constructive to character and edifying to spiritual life."*

It is crucial that you understand who you are in God's eyes, how precious you are to Him, how He now sees you (as the result of what Jesus did, through His sacrifice on the cross). You must understand what it means to have Jesus as a mediator between you and God; having rendered you completely blameless by His sacrifice on the cross, and freely giving you all things in accordance with God's will and purpose for your life and your calling.

So be yourself; but in Christ, and stop trying to "behave" your way into God's favour; just accept it! It's the "being in Christ", along with the goodness of God, that will cause your behaviour to change; not so that you can get more stuff from God; but for your benefit alone. For as the influences of your flesh decrease; the way is clear for spiritual knowledge and understanding, and the leading of the Holy Spirit to increase.

1 Peter 1:13 (Amp) "So brace up your minds; be sober (circumspect, morally alert); set your hope wholly and unchangeably on the grace (divine flavour) that is coming to you when Jesus Christ (the Messiah) is revealed." There are great gains from having a revelation of who Jesus Christ really is, and who you are in Him! 2 Peter 1:2

The New Testament scriptures relating to our behaviour are not laws. The New Testament scriptures relate to the teachings under the new covenant of grace.

Galatians 5:18 (KJV) "But if ye be led of the Spirit, ye are not under the law." Sinful behaviour won't stop a believer from going to heaven, but depending on what it is, it could have a less than positive and a less than God ordained effect on your life, and in worst cases, could even wreak havoc in your life here on earth. There's one thing to go through the trials we face in life that are allowed by God, meant as a tool for shaping our character; however, it's another thing to go through trials as a result of our own sinful choices. God's grace is available to keep us; however, we should avoid "leaning-in" (yielding) to our fallen nature willfully or deliberately, or with deliberate insidiousness; thereby, tempting Christ by taking His grace for granted.

The behavioural instructions; therefore, given to us in the New Testament scriptures (under the new covenant of Grace) are for our good, because the less your mind is cluttered with the influences of your flesh; the easier it will be for you to hear and to see the leading of the Holy Spirit, so that you may experience the fullness of the purpose of God in your life here on earth, before you go to be with Him in heaven.

If you are in Christ, God does not punish you when your behaviour is contrary to righteousness. See this, and see it very clearly: No matter how good you may think you are, no matter how sinless you may think your life is; if the sacrifice of Christ is removed from you, your "good-deeds-doing-self" will not receive eternal life in heaven! Period! You cannot earn your way into heaven by what you do, or don't do! There's absolutely nothing you can do, or not do, that qualifies you as righteous from God's perspective! The sacrifice of Jesus is the only thing that makes you righteous!

So if you are in Christ, why would God punish you for sins that he no longer sees or acknowledges?! Why would God punish you as if you were still under the Old Covenant Law?! Is God a liar?! Has the Cross failed?! Absolutely not!! So, just in case I haven't made myself clear, GOD-DOES-NOT-PUNISH-THOSE-WHO-ARE-IN-CHRIST! It's the choices that we make in ignorance of our new delivered state, that cause troubles in our our lives; but even in that, the Word of God says, **Romans 8:28 (KJV) *"And we know that all things work together for good to them that love God, to them who are the called according to His purpose."*** "All things" means ALL THINGS! Not just the good choices you make! Oh wouldn't it be wonderful if every single decision we ever make was just perfect?! We are flawed; all of us! This is why the grace of God is so awesome! God can even cause our mess to work out for our good! The key, is to allow yourself (even in your mess) to be led of the Holy Spirit! In so doing, you will never be in a bad situation where there is no way of escape (even if it's of your own doing!), and those types of situations will be for your spiritual learning, and for the development of your character.

We can do nothing (in this life) to separate ourselves from our sinful nature; as Paul demonstrates in Romans chapter

7. Our sinful nature shall remain with us always; however, a person with understanding (a wise person) would habitually make choices that are in alignment with their new righteous nature rather than choices influenced by their sinful nature. The pleasures you enjoy by pleasing your flesh cannot, and will never come close to the fullness of pleasures in Christ. The question is, are you willing to subdue your flesh and be surrendered to your new righteous nature.

In you (those who are in Christ) exists two natures, two versions of yourself: your fallen nature (your flesh), and your new righteous nature in Christ. If you find your Christian journey challenging, difficult and tiresome; if it's a struggle for you to keep your thoughts, words, and your actions consistent with your new righteous nature, so in exasperation, you find yourself saying, "I just wanna be myself!"; I encourage you to think about what you're saying. Which version of "Myself" do you want to be? Choose wisely!

God never stops speaking to you, and He never stops showing you; you just can't hear Him through all of life's noise, and you can't see Him through all of life's clutter.

CHAPTER 7

I Just Don't Believe!

"If God is real, why is there so much pain and suffering in the world?" There are multiple reasons why people ask questions like this; however, often they're either people who really would like to believe (and are generally agnostic); however, (amongst other things) they feel a sense of hopelessness by what they perceive to be unchecked cruelty in the world, and the conflicts amongst world religions, coupled with destructive ideologies doesn't exactly help. On the other hand; there are those who deliberately look for reasons not to believe in God. For the latter, the motives behind their unbelief could be related to one, or several things; such as unresolved anger or resentment (due to troubles in their own personal lives), or rebellion against religion in general for fear of losing their free will, and being forced to conform to religious laws. Their reasons could be because of unresolved hurts or disappointments, or their unwillingness to accept anything that hasn't been proven by science (which is sad considering how grossly lacking humanity is in our understanding of things here on earth; let alone the universe and beyond). In the end, it could just be plain hate, and so on, and so on. People's reasons for not believing in God could be for any, or all of these reasons; nonetheless, whatever their reasons, it causes them to seek answers for their's and the world's problems from the very source responsible for them, humanity!

To people who are deliberately looking for reasons not to believe, the Word of God says: **Romans 1:20 (Amp)** ***For ever since the creation of the world His invisible nature and attributes, that is, His eternal power and divinity, have been made intelligible and clearly discernible in and through the things that have been made (His handiworks). So men are without excuse altogether without any defence or justification.***

Now for those who want to believe, but are just troubled by what they see and hear in the world; you just haven't been speaking to the right people, and perhaps this book will help you; however, like I said from the beginning, I'm not trying to convert anyone; I'm just here to deliver the truth, so it's entirely up to you what you decide to do from here.

Now some may ask why I refer to what I believe as "truth"; it's because of free will. It's my free will to believe, as much as it is yours not to; nonetheless, God is sovereign, and doesn't require any of us to believe, for Him to be real. As for me; I choose to believe, and I can strongly testify with deep understanding as to the benefits of my belief.

So this will make for a very short chapter, because everything you need to see, hear, or feel has already been revealed to you by God (Romans 1:20). Whether you acknowledge it or not is on you; however, I know from experience that God is good (to all of us), and He gives everyone with the ability to reason, the opportunity to know that He is real.

Mark 10:13-14 (KJV) [13] "And they brought young children to him, that he should touch them: and His disciples rebuked those that brought them. [14] But when Jesus saw it, he was much displeased, and said unto them, Suffer the little children to come unto me, and forbid them not: for of such is the kingdom of God."

As for those who aren't able discern God's existence through the evidence of creation; for instance little children, or infants, or those who (being mentally challenged) are like children; God's grace covers them for they have no knowledge of good or evil (Deuteronomy 1:39), and if they should die, they will go to heaven (just to clear that up). So God does not exclude anyone from receiving or accepting salvation. Absolutely anyone who accepts that Jesus Christ was sacrificed on their behalf, will be received by God, and will reap the benefits thereof, which includes being saved from spending eternity in a realm that was never meant for humanity; instead, created by God for Satan (the devil) and the third of the host of angels, who rebelled against God, and were cast out of heaven (Revelation 12:7-9).

All the effective and lasting solutions to your personal problems, and the problems of the world in general are all in God through Jesus Christ; however, you have to believe in God to receive the solutions, and to become the solution.

Finally, please do not be deceived, troubled or deterred from your pursuit of truth by people professing to be Christians; however, their words, attitude, prejudices and hatred paints a completely opposite picture. The Bible says you will know the disciples of Jesus by their fruit: ***Matthew 7:15-20 (KJV) [15] "Beware of false prophets, which come to you in sheep's clothing, but inwardly they are ravening wolves. [16] Ye shall know them by their fruits. Do men gather grapes of thorns, or figs of thistles? [17] Even so every good tree bringeth forth good fruit; but a corrupt tree bringeth forth evil fruit. [18] A good tree cannot bring forth evil fruit, neither can a corrupt tree bring forth good fruit. [19] Every tree that***

bringeth not forth good fruit is hewn down, and cast into the fire. [20] Wherefore by their fruits ye shall know them. " The thing is, you have to know the true nature of Jesus to know whether someone is truly His disciple or not. Again, hopefully in some way, this book will help.

Nuff said.

If we recognise God's grace in all things and be forever grateful, our spirit will be forever comforted and we'll never add anxiety to a day already filled with evil.

CHAPTER 8

What Ails You?

When making the distinction between ourselves and God the Father, the Son and the Holy Spirit; it's important that we are not just aware, but honest about our particular weaknesses and flaws, which are indicative of our fallen nature. Why is this important? Because so many Christians are supposedly doing or saying things in the name of Jesus that's got absolutely nothing to do with God, Jesus, or the Holy Spirit. This is because they really don't know Jesus, if they did; they would see that their thoughts, or words, or behaviour is inconsistent with the character and nature of Jesus, and they would change their ways. On the other hand, deceitfulness and the desire for control comes into play when people are actually aware of the true essence of Jesus (the scriptures are right there for them to read); however, they refuse to acknowledge, or accept that their perspective, attitude or behaviour is inconsistent with the character of Christ. Now this is just downright evil; but sadly a real and unfortunate situation in life, because there are so many people who are put off from allowing God into their lives because of what they see and hear from people professing to be Christians; but they lack the true essence of the one who is the originator of unconditional love. ***2 Timothy 3:5 (Amp) "For [although] they hold a form of piety (true religion), they deny and reject and are strangers to the power of it [their conduct belies the genuineness of their profession]. Avoid [all] such people, [turn away from them]."***

So what can we do to ensure we do well in representing Jesus amongst those around us, and in the world at large? We can start by being honest about our flaws. ***James 5:16 (KJV) "Confess your faults one to another...",*** This does not mean, "Confess your sins", as many people misinterpret it to mean. Our sins are already forgiven (past, present and future). We don't even have to confess our sins to Jesus; He already knows about them! Being innocent, pure, holy, blameless, and without fault, yet dying a painful death on the cross for the sins of all humanity, is not something you easily forget!

God never even asked us for an apology before He forgave us! ***Romans 5:8 (Amp) "But God shows and clearly proves His own love for us by the fact that while we were still sinners, Christ (the Messiah, the Anointed One) died for us."*** What James 5:16 means is that we are to be honest with one another (and with ourselves) about our faults, our flaws. Having said that; however, it's as the situation or circumstance requires, as the Holy Spirit leads; you don't go blabbing your business to any random person, Christian or otherwise!

How do you identify and rise above your flaws? Good question. I'm glad you asked. I spent eleven and a half years in the United States Air Force. When I was in basic training, the primary goal of my drill instructor was to "drive" the civilian out of me by attacking (what could be considered) that part of my character, and making me feel like a worthless "puke" (as they called us). Once he got it into my head that my civilian nature, disposition, attitude, or anything civilian about me was as good as "puke" to the military; then he would start building me back up; but into a lean, mean military machine! This; however, never would've worked without my cooperation. I had to accept that I would be ineffective as an Airman, if I held on to my civilian nature, attitude or disposition. I had to reject my old behaviour, my old nature, and embrace a new one, and I had to do this willingly; otherwise, my experience in basic training would have been bad, really bad. There were indeed men in my squadron who resisted the training, even rebelled against it; but they were either set back to retrain again in certain areas (which of course prolonged their stay in basic training) or they were simply kicked out of the military.

Two weeks into my basic military training, I remember lying in my bunk at "lights-out" and thinking to myself, "What have I gotten myself into?!" Then I remembered what my older brother (Ricky) said to me who also served in the Airforce; he said, "The drill instructor is doing what he must do to make you effective as an Airman; do not take it personally!" I remembered this, embraced it, and it changed absolutely everything!

From that night onwards, I realised that the training I was receiving was simply stripping away everything about me (inside and out) that was fearful, messy, or lazy, and was helping me to be laser focused on becoming courageous and excellent in every aspect of my character. Such was my enthusiasm from that night onwards, that I was promoted to second in command; i.e., when my drill instructor wasn't around, I was in charge! That was a really big deal in basic training! All because I surrendered to the will of my drill instructor, and allowed my civilian related flaws, fears and weaknesses to be exposed as character traits that would hinder my success as an Airforce Airman. I allowed them to be purged, and I embraced the pursuit of military excellence instead. I absolutely loved every moment of my military basic training from that night until graduating. I also loved all of the eleven and a half years afterwards, until I left the Airforce in response to the leading of the Holy Spirit.

Before joining the military, I never knew how much of a better person I could be. The wonderful thing is; the essence of who I am, that deep inner core, that soil from which a good version, or a bad version of myself is cultivated, never changed; it was just fed the right nutrients which allowed a better version of myself to blossom. After basic training, and technical training school, my life in the Airforce became very much (in routine) like civilian life, I went to work, did my job and went home; that was pretty much it. When I was off duty, I was able to pursue my personal interests with a tenacity, focus and determination that I didn't have prior to basic military training; but again, it was because I made a freewill choice to embrace the military training; that's what made the difference!

Similarly, as a Christian, you must be willing to abandon your old ways (however comfortable they may be to you), and embrace being rebuilt in the image of Jesus. (I mean the clue is in the word, "Christ-ian"; i.e, Christ-like!) In so doing, not only will the "journey" expose the corrosive areas in your life, but it will teach you how to overcome them, and grow beyond them. If you don't; however, understand and embrace what God is desiring to achieve in and through you; then your journey as a Christian will be hard, and it will be painful, and just like military basic training you'll experience setback after setback; having to go through the same trials over and over again, until they have the life changing, character building effect on you, as intended by God.

2 Timothy 3:16 (KJV) "All scripture is given by inspiration of God, and is profitable for doctrine, for reproof, for correction, for instruction in righteousness."

Do your thoughts, words and actions align with the teachings in the scriptures? The New Testament scriptures in particular (as they are given to us under the new covenant of grace) are important to the Christian because they speak of us being delivered from the old covenant Law of God, and instead being led by the Holy Spirit regarding how we should think, speak and behave, that we may be the best version of ourselves; however, all the scriptures of the Bible collectively, give us complete insight to God and His relationship with humanity. The scriptures will show you what you could be, but you have to be willing to be honest about your flaws, and surrender your will to the will of God; trusting that He only wants the absolute best for you, exceedingly above all you could ask or think.

So what ails you? Whatever it is, are you willing to surrender it to become a better version of yourself? Your effectiveness in the world as a Christian will be determined by the extent to which you (in your daily life) are able to reflect the love and grace of Jesus upon others (all people unconditionally and without prejudice), your ability to embrace the essence of Jesus and apply it to all the areas of your life, and finally; but not least, your sensitivity to the leading of the Holy Spirit, who will guide you in all situations. All this; however, hinges totally upon your willingness to identify; then surrender to God, the areas of your life which are inconsistent with the true nature of Jesus, and your willingness to allow God (the ultimate drill instructor) to rebuild you anew.

A person who shouts, "Look how successful I am" may have stuff; but is not truly successful.

CHAPTER 9

Wisdom

Proverbs 9:10 (KJV) *"The fear of the Lord is the beginning of wisdom: and the knowledge of the holy is understanding."* The Word "fear" in this context does not mean fear as in "afraid"; it means worshipful reverence of God in acknowledgment of His infinite and almighty power, His unmeasurable greatness, and His absolute sovereignty over His creation. **Romans 9:21 (KJV)** *"Hath not the potter power over the clay, of the same lump to make one vessel unto honour, and another unto dishonour?"* This scripture is important because it puts into perspective the sovereign authority of God to create, and to destroy in accordance with His will, and in fulfilment of His purpose. A sculptor creates one sculpture for one purpose, and another sculpture for a different purpose, or he may decide to destroy them both, and start all over; such is the sculptor's complete authority to do so. Amp this up by say, ten trillion, trillion, trillion, and you still won't come even close to the absolute sovereignty, power and authority possessed by God over His creation. This is why we should "fear" Him.

So why is this "fear" the beginning of wisdom? When we choose to worship God in acknowledgement of His greatness, when we seek to know Him by surrendering our lives to Him, allowing Him to order our steps; we obtain access to everything we require to be victorious in every situation and circumstance that confronts us in life. That choice, right there, is the beginning of wisdom.

You don't have to believe in God to have wisdom; however, God is the author of wisdom; its originating source; therefore, any wisdom emanating from the creation's mouth, flows from the Creator, and with God, there is no lacking, or depletion of wisdom. When we; therefore, surrender our lives to God, we have access to all wisdom, and we are not limited to only that which we can perceive on our own.

True wisdom (which is the wisdom of God) gives you the ability to make decisions or choices, in any given situation, that are consistent with the will of God. If you already "fear" the Lord, and you already have knowledge of him; then you already have wisdom, and you possess understanding. All you're required to do now is to simply have confidence in this scripture (Proverbs 9:10), and know that as you remain surrendered to the leading of the Holy Spirit, you will never put a foot wrong. When I say, "You will never put a foot wrong", I mean never! Why? Because God says, He will order your steps. **Psalm 37:23-26 (KJV) [23]** *"The steps of a good man are ordered by the Lord : and he delighteth in his way. [24] Though he fall, he shall not be utterly cast down: for the Lord upholdeth him with His hand. [25] I have been young, and now am old; yet have I not seen the righteous forsaken, nor his seed begging bread. [26] He is ever merciful, and lendeth; and his seed is blessed."*

Is God a liar? Absolutely not! So why should you be concerned about not having the wisdom to make good decisions?! The only thing that will most certainly cause you to make decisions that are inconsistent with the will of God (causing you to struggle), is fear and doubt, and more specifically; doubting that you (who are in Christ) already have access to all wisdom! Remember what the Word of God says here: **Romans 8:28 (KJV)** *"And we know that all things work together for good to them that love God, to them who are the called according to His purpose."* You can't put a foot wrong! God will make it work out for you! So whatever you step into, just trust God, and be led by the Holy Spirit; if you're not where you're meant to be, God will lead you out of it; but even in that situation, you won't come out empty handed. Why? Because even in our so called "wrong" choices; there is something to be gained from it; that is, if we listen to the Holy Spirit.

If you've accepted Jesus Christ into your life; then your position with God has been restored, and you should expect all the benefits that come with that restoration. ***Colossians 2:9 (KJV) "For in him dwelleth all the fulness of the Godhead bodily."***

The gospel says that you are in Christ, and that Christ is in you, which means, you are seated with Christ at the right hand of God, and the fullness of God dwells in you. This is a great opportunity for an illustration:

Being in Christ, and having Christ in you, is like taking a glass of water, and putting it into a bucket of water. Now when you do that, the water in the glass becomes mixed with the water in the bucket, and the water in the bucket becomes mixed with the water in the glass. In fact, the water in the glass becomes indistinguishable from the water in the bucket! Now replace the water in the glass with your spirit, and the water in the bucket with the Spirit of Christ. This is why when God looks at those who are in Christ; all He sees is Christ! How much more convincing do you need before you accept that you already have wisdom and understanding! Not your own wisdom or your own understanding, but the wisdom and understanding of God Himself! Yeah, I said it! How can Christ, who is God made flesh, dwell in you and you in Him, and you not have access to all wisdom?!

God is in you, so you already have wisdom; you simply have to access it! How? By faith! *Isaiah 30:21 (KJV) "And thine ears shall hear a word behind thee, saying, This is the way, walk ye in it, when ye turn to the right hand, and when ye turn to the left."*

If you listen to that inner voice, the Holy Spirit will give you wisdom for every situation and circumstance you face in life. *Psalm 32:8-9 (Amp) [8] "I the Lord will instruct you and teach you in the way you should go; I will counsel you with My eye upon you. [9] Be not like the horse or the mule, which lack understanding, which must have their mouths held firm with bit and bridle, or else they will not come with you."* Do not allow fear to paralyse you; fear is a faith killer and a purpose killer! Do not be afraid to move forward, or be fearful about what to do; just step, and let God do the rest.

There are a multitude of sins in the world; hate, malice, greed, divisiveness, deceitfulness, lies, false prophets spewing false doctrines, and a cornucopia of corrosive enticements appealing specifically (by default) to our flesh; all of which are "purpose" destroying obstacles. So here's the deal:

Wisdom

Love covers the multitude of sins (1 Peter 4:8); but wisdom gives you the ability to navigate through them.

God measures our love for Him by how we treat each other.

CHAPTER 10

"Free at last, Free at Last..."

There is a thread that runs through this entire book, weaving in and out of every chapter, you may have already identified it; that thread is freedom. The most important aspect of your relationship with God, through Christ, is that you are now free from the bondages of sin, and you are at peace with God. In this chapter I would like to help you understand what makes you free, and how your response to it could lead others to freedom.

Many people associate freedom with the possession of wealth. Having great wealth gives you the freedom to buy whatever you like; but is that it? Is freedom defined by how many purchases you can make? Really?! I'm not even remotely suggesting that you should be broke, absolutely not.

What I'm saying is this: One person has accumulated, or has inherited great wealth, and the thought of losing it terrifies the person, so the person is insecure but boastful, self-centred, short tempered, ruthless in their business dealings, dishonest, selfish in giving, lacking in integrity, paranoid with regards to relationships; and so on, you get the picture. Another person has accumulated, or inherited great wealth, and is grateful to have it; but, the wealth is not the source of their contentment; in fact, the person was content before becoming wealthy. This person is confident; but humble, selfless, patient, generous and wise in their business dealings, truthful, philanthropic in giving, trustworthy and trusting of others. Which person is free? Is freedom defined by what you have, or by who you are?

I know of many people who have great wealth, however their lives are filled with misery, and even despair. I'd like to suggest to you that freedom, is defined by who you are.

Romans 7:15 (KJV) "For that which I do I allow not: for what I would, that do I not; but what I hate, that do I." Remember this scripture from earlier in the book? Before you think you're experiencing déjà vu; I'm using this scripture and a few others from earlier in the book to make a similar, but different point. So again; what the Apostle Paul is talking about here is him doing the (sinful) things he desires not to do; however, this does not mean that Paul missed out on heaven, as would be the case for the people described in Galatians 5:19-21.

Again, as we discussed earlier, Paul further explains that it's not actually him that's doing it, but sin in him. The great Apostle Paul, with sin in him?! Nooooo! Read on... **Romans 7:20 (Amp) *"Now if I do what I do not desire to do, it is no longer I doing it [it is not myself that acts], but the sin [principle] which dwells within me [fixed and operating in my soul]."*** In Romans 7:25 Paul says, ***"With the mind I myself serve the law of God, but with the flesh the law of sin.»*** Paul says further in Galatians 5:18 (Amp), ***"But if you are guided (led) by the [Holy] Spirit, you are not subject to the Law"*** which, as mentioned earlier, means neither can we be condemned by the Law. Remember, the old covenant Law judges those who have not accepted their salvation, given freely by God, through Jesus Christ.

Again, to recap: What we see in Galatians 5:18, is that those of us who have accepted our salvation through Jesus Christ, have received grace, which is the unmerited favour of God. It means that, in spite of our sinful nature, we (because of our faith in Jesus Christ) are seen by God as righteous; meaning, we have been set free from the condemnation of the Law. Now hold on, before you throw off all inhibitions, and start whoopin' it up, and gettin' your freak on, please read on... ***Galatians 5:13 (Amp) "For you, brethren, were indeed called to freedom; only do not let your freedom be an incentive to your flesh and an opportunity or excuse for selfishness, but through love you should serve one another."*** Here it is again: ***1 Corinthians 6:12 (Amp)***

"Everything is permissible (allowable and lawful) for me; but not all things are helpful (good for me to do, expedient and profitable when considered with other things). Everything is lawful for me, but I will not become the slave of anything or be brought under its power." And just in case you still didn't get it, it's repeated again here: ***1 Corinthians 10:23 (Amp) "All things are legitimate, permissible and we are free to do anything we please, but not all things are helpful (expedient, profitable, and wholesome). All things are legitimate, but not all things are constructive to character and edifying to spiritual life."***

Yes, you are free; however, in your freedom, love and wisdom is required. If you truly are in Christ, He died for you once and for all. Jesus doesn't get back on the cross and sacrifice himself over and over again every time your behaviour is inconsistent with righteousness! If you; therefore, are in Christ, what you say, think, or do will not cause you to go to hell; however, it may cause you or someone else to suffer here on earth. Check this out: ***1 John 3:17-23 (KJV)*** *[17]*

"Free at last, Free at Last..."

"But whoso hath this world's good, and seeth his brother have need, and shutteth up his bowels of compassion from him, how dwelleth the love of God in him? [18] My little children, let us not love in word, neither in tongue; but in deed and in truth. [19] And hereby we know that we are of the truth, and shall assure our hearts before him. [20] For if our heart condemn us, God is greater than our heart, and knoweth all things. [21] Beloved, if our heart condemn us not, then have we confidence toward God. [22] And whatsoever we ask, we receive of Him, because we keep His commandments, and do those things that are pleasing in His sight." If your heart is free from condemnation (which it should be if you are in Christ); then you won't insult the grace of God by going around thinking that you have to behave a certain way to just to get stuff from God; i.e., earn His blessings. *1 John 17:23 "And this is His commandment, That we should believe on the name of His Son Jesus Christ, and love one another, as he gave us commandment."* Our behaviour towards one another should be motivated by love, period, plain and simple; not so that we can get stuff from God! Love activates your desire to think, say, and do that which is pleasing to God, and edifying to one another; whilst wisdom gives us the means by which to do so. That fact is, you are in Christ; therefore, seek to understand what that means, and have confidence in that. God loves you and will not forsake you.

James 4:2-3 (KJV) [2] "Ye lust, and have not: ye kill, and desire to have, and cannot obtain: ye fight and war, yet ye have not, because ye ask not. [3] Ye ask, and receive not, because ye ask amiss, that ye may consume it upon your lusts."

This speaks about people (who are obviously not in Christ) asking God for things; but not receiving them because their asking is corrupted by ungodly intentions. It states that if they were to receive what they've asked for; it would be consumed upon their lusts; i.e., spent on things to satisfy their sinful nature. This is why it's so important to be firmly rooted in Christ, and be led by the Holy Spirit, so that your "asking" may be consistent with the will of God. James 4:2-3 is important to understand because God has no desire to facilitate or finance your destruction.

Here's another thing to be aware of; because people tend to freak out when troubles or difficulties come their way: The trials you go through in life are meant to mould your character, so that the things God has purposed you to have, will not only be a blessing to you; but to others as well. So you should ask yourself, what is the motivation behind your asking? At the very least, your asking should be motivated by your desire to see the manifestation of what you already believe, or know to be the will of God for you in that situation; in accordance with His Word. Also, ask with the knowledge that you have been set free from the condemnation of sin,

"Free at last, Free at Last..."

so that your asking may be with confidence. ***Hebrews 4:16 (KJV) "Let us therefore come boldly unto the throne of grace, that we may obtain mercy, and find grace to help in time of need."*** "...Come boldly..." This mindset helps to set you free from the condemnation and guilt of sin; drawing you even closer to God.

Matthew 6:33 (KJV) "But seek ye first the kingdom of God, and His righteousness; and all these things shall be added unto you." The more mature, grounded, steadfast and secure your spiritual life is (your relationship with God), the easier it becomes for you to be led by the Holy Spirit rather than your sinful nature; to the end that you might receive from God, by His divine grace, that which you ask, in accordance to His will, and walk in power and authority; whilst experiencing the fulfilment of the purpose of God in, and for your life here on earth.

This chapter about being free is important, because a lot of Christians are struggling with feelings of condemnation and unworthiness. Why? Because they are being told by the "self-righteous", that their "sins" are stopping the blessings of God from flowing in their lives; so they're running around trying to be good enough for God to bless them; all the while, their hearts condemn them. So they struggle. Now the self-righteous will experience unnecessary troubles and hardships as well. Why? Because...well...because they're self-righteous!

So what makes you free? Remember, if you are in Christ, you have been set free from the guilt and condemnation of sin; therefore, you don't have to try to be "good" to receive what God has purposed you to to have. In fact, trying to be "good" to get God to move on your behalf is an insult to Jesus' sacrifice on the cross, it is an insult to the grace of God. God doesn't need your "good", He needs your faith in grace! We can never be good enough to earn the blessings of God! Those who try, insult the Holy Spirit and the grace of God! The blessings of God are gifted to us by His grace! God is neither increased, nor decreased by your behaviour! Please don't get me wrong; by all means, let the righteousness of God be reflected in your thoughts, words and actions; not to impress God, or anyone else for that matter, but to this end; that your righteous behaviour might be edifying to others (encouraging them), because you might be the only "Jesus" someone else may ever see.

Above all, please remember that if you have received Jesus into your heart; God now sees you as righteous. You are free from from sin, and the debilitating and corrosive nature of it. So as you, with truth and earnest, engage in the never ending battle against your flesh to walk in your new righteous nature; God is always and forever good, merciful, forgiving, gracious, patient and kind.

What you say you want is not what you really want, what you really want is determined by what you're saying.

CHAPTER 11

Managing Your Expectations

In this chapter, I'd like to help you dissect your expectations to determine whether your thoughts, words and actions are truly in sync with what you say your expecting. Most people desire to live a comfortable life; however, is that truly what they're expecting? I say, "most people" because some of us just want the will of God to be fulfilled in us and through us, "comfortable" is relative, but we'll get to that later.

__Jeremiah 29:11 (KJV)__ "For I know the thoughts that I think toward you, saith the Lord, thoughts of peace, and not of evil,

Managing Your Expectations

to give you an expected end." What are your expectations? Whatever they are, you will have what you expect. Now this applies whether your expectations are good, or bad because you will draw to yourself that which you are truly expecting, regardless of what you may say you're expecting.

So how do you know what your true expectations are? Here's an exercise: Think about when you cross a busy road. You look both ways then, when you see that it's safe to cross, you do so without any concern as to whether you'll make it safely to the other side. You, in that moment, truly expect to safely get to the other side of that road. Here's another: Let's say you go for a job interview. Now before the interview, you pray and ask God to give you the job; however, after the interview you worry about whether you got the job or not, and you say something like, "oh, they probably won't give me the job."

The former example demonstrates true expectation; when I say "true", I mean at the subconscious level. In the former example, if you think about the thought process that influenced the action of crossing the road with confidence that you'll make it to the other side without getting run over; that's what it feels like to truly expect something. In other words, you absolutely know what you're expecting will come to pass; and that absolute assurance, that true expectation, is validated by your actions and by your words.

The latter example demonstrates what it's like to say or think you're expecting something; when actually (subconsciously) you're not. That's not to say that if you don't have confidence in yourself; then you won't receive that which you desire; just make sure you continue to have confidence and faith in God! God is gracious, and He is sovereign; so it may be God's will that you receive that which you desire, just to draw your attention to His goodness and grace; so that you may learn to trust Him in spite of the lack of confidence you may have in your own ability. However, a person who consistently doubts whether they will receive that which they say they are expecting, will most likely not receive it at all.

James 1:5-8 (KJV) [5] "If any of you lack wisdom, let him ask of God, that giveth to all men liberally, and upbraideth not; and it shall be given him. [6] But let him ask in faith, nothing wavering. For he that wavereth is like a wave of the sea driven with the wind and tossed. [7] For let not that man think that he shall receive any thing of the Lord. [8] A double minded man is unstable in all his ways." In these scriptures, James speaks about asking God for wisdom, but the same applies to anything you ask God for. The job interview example I gave earlier demonstrates someone who is double minded.

Let's pause here, and put some things straight, so that we're not putting the cart before the horse. Referencing Jeremiah 29:11, what are God's desires (expectations) for you? That's what you should be expecting. So before you go off on tangent, expecting to find a genie in a lamp, or a pot of gold at the end of a rainbow; ask yourself, "what does God want for me?" First of all, whatever it is, it will be good for you. Now "Good for you", doesn't necessarily mean fun and pleasurable. It might be painful; but it will be good for you nonetheless because (in spite of what you may think) God knows exactly what you have need of in any given situation. You; therefore, may need to go through this painful process just so that the thing that's hindering your blessing may be purged from you!

Any fitness instructor will tell you, "no pain, no gain!". So what's good for you may not necessarily be pleasurable. This is why it's so necessary to know the will of God for you (what God expects for you), because if it's not necessarily pleasurable, at least you'll know that it's God's will; which means you can take comfort in the fact that, in spite of the pain, you know you'll be better off for it. As Jeremiah 29:11 says, God's desires for you are of peace and not evil.

Romans 8:28 (KJV) "And we know that all things work together for good to them that love God, to them who are the called according to His purpose." When life seems painful, please remember what God says in this verse. The scripture says, "all things"; not just the good stuff! That said, when you're in the will of God; it's all good stuff! No matter what it looks like (if you trust God), good will come of it! When you're in Christ, things happen "for" you, not "to" you! ***Romans 5:3-4 (Amp) [3] Moreover let us also be full of joy now! Let us exult and triumph in our troubles and rejoice in our sufferings, knowing that pressure and affliction and hardship produce patient and unswerving endurance. [4] And endurance (fortitude) develops maturity of character (approved faith and tried integrity). And character of this sort produces the habit of joyful and confident hope of eternal salvation."***

It would be wise for you to do what we are instructed to do in Romans 5:3-4. Here's another one: ***James 1:2-4 (Amp) [2] "Consider it wholly joyful, my brethren, whenever you are enveloped in or encounter trials of any sort or fall into various temptations. [3] Be assured and understand that the trial and proving of your faith bring out endurance and steadfastness and patience. [4] But let endurance and steadfastness and patience have full play and do a thorough work, so that you may be people perfectly and fully developed with no defects, lacking in nothing."***

You may say, "I just lost a loved one, why on earth would God want me to rejoice in this situation?!" Why? Because even death is not bigger than the love, grace, goodness, mercy, and power of God! Whilst we're on the topic; let me just add this: Death is inevitable, and should not have the "chokehold" on you that it has. God is bigger! The traumatising effect death has on the living is an extremely good reason to have a strong relationship with God; for when death comes calling in the life of the person who is strong in Christ; it will not destroy them, and the way you handle yourself in the face of death will be a testimony to the love and power of God; giving strength and hope to those around you.

So what is God's will for you? What does God want you to have? *Matthew 6:31-33 (KJV) [31] "Therefore take no thought, saying, What shall we eat? or, What shall we drink? or, Wherewithal shall we be clothed? [32] (For after all these things do the Gentiles seek:) for your heavenly Father knoweth that ye have need of all these things. [33] But seek ye first the kingdom of God, and His righteousness; and all these things shall be added unto you."* If you read from Matthew 6:25, Jesus is instructing us not to worry about acquiring stuff; whether it be a house to live in, clothes to wear, or food to eat; all the stuff we seek so that we may be "comfortable". What Jesus is saying in these verses is: if God can look after the birds, and even the mere grass in the fields, how much more will He look after you!

God wants you to have all things that relate to His Kingdom, and His righteousness; which covers absolutely everything you could possibly need in life. That of itself equates to comfort, which is one of the reasons why God says, rejoice in your trials. At no point in your life should circumstances suck the joy of the Lord from your heart, or steal your comfort. You are in Christ, and Christ is in God which means, you have the full power of God within you! You should stop and think about this! I'll wait here...

You got it now? Can you see it?! When you do; anything life throws at you will neither hinder, nor destroy what God has purposed you to have!

I've digressed; what was I saying? Oh yeah - What does God want you to have?

There is a great and powerful peace that comes from knowing what God wants for you. Such is the power of that peace (or conviction), that not even circumstances, or situations which may suggest to the contrary, will be able to disquiet your mind! To obtain; however, this level of conviction in your expectations, you must not allow your present circumstances to discourage you. ***Philippians 4:11 (KJV) "Not that I speak in respect of want: for I have learned, in whatsoever state I am, therewith to be content."*** Whatever state you find yourself in, be content. Why? Because the acquisition of your expectations should never be the source of your peace! You should never say (or think), "I'll be happy when I have..." or "I'll be happy when I get..." God and only God should be the source of your peace, contentment, happiness, joy, etc. Why? (Wow, you with the questions!) I'll tell you why. First, have a read of these scriptures: ***Matthew 6:19-21***

(Amp) [19] "Do not gather and heap up and store up for yourselves treasures on earth, where moth and rust and worm consume and destroy, and where thieves break through and steal. [20] But gather and heap up and store for yourselves treasures in heaven, where neither moth nor rust nor worm consume and destroy, and where thieves do not break through and steal; [21] For where your treasure is, there will your heart be also."

As the result of the fall of Jim Bakker's PTL ministry in the late 1980's, many Christians lost their faith. This was because their heart was in their tangible "treasure", here on earth, and that "treasure", to them, was Jim Bakker and his PTL ministry; or more accurately, what they believed they could get from God in return for their financial contribution and their support for Jim Bakker and his PTL ministry. When Jim Bakker fell, and subsequently PTL; to many people, that equated to the loss of whatever they were expecting from God.

When Jesus says you should store for yourself treasures in heaven, He's talking about having faith in God, because in so doing, you store non-perishable treasures for yourself in heaven; things like unconditional love, peace, joy, forgiveness, grace, wisdom, understanding, patience, contentment, gratitude, strength of character, help in a time of need, etc. All the things that keep you from losing your mind when you lose those perishable things you've stored up for yourself here on earth!

Let's say you've worked really hard for years, and you finally buy that house, or that car you've longed for. How would you feel if it were damaged or destroyed by a flood, or a fire, or if it was vandalised in some way? Would you be devastated? Be honest. Maybe you already have lost something, or someone, or you've suffered or you're currently suffering through an illness; are you still truly joyful, grateful, at peace, etc.? These may seem weighty questions for weighty examples; but I've seen a person "lose it" just because someone spilled a little bit of fluid on his clothes!

When you place value on perishable things (or even people) here on earth, to the point where if they were lost or damaged, you would "lose it"; then you make yourself vulnerable to life itself, forever being a victim, and the more you lose, the deeper you sink into dark places. Life is full of losses, so with that in mind; it is wise to store for yourself treasures in heaven by placing your faith in God from whom all the things synonymous with Jesus and the Kingdom of Heaven flows.

I love my wife, Paula, so deeply that there are no words that could possibly do my feelings for her any justice; however, my faith is not in my wife; it's in God! So if it's God's will that I'm still alive when Paula passes from this life to be with Christ; God, Jesus, the Holy Spirit and all the heavenly "treasures" I possess from knowing them will still be available to me here on earth! I will; therefore, remain sober in my spirit, which will enable me to be a pillar of strength for my children and for others to lean on, who share my loss. That would honour Paula; me being devastated by losing her would not.

"Therman, are you saying I shouldn't be upset if I lose a loved one?!" Of course you should be upset; I would! I; however, would not be upset to the point of devastation, where I'm just no use to anyone, or anything! As it is, there is no pleasure in death for those left behind; therefore, I refuse to give victory to death by being defeated in the face of it! Now you can if you want to, that's your choice; but does that bring the person back? Does your total devastation somehow honour the person? Would the person you lost be pleased and delighted that you're shattered, broken and despairing? Of course not; not if they loved you! What good is accomplished by both the loss of a loved one, and your devastation by that loss? How does your devastation help those who love you, who are still living? The scriptures say we should "mourn with those who mourn" (Rom 12:15 NIV). This of course, means to show empathy, which is proper and good; but that's all it means because what good are you to anyone who is grieving, if you're as devastated as they are?!

So what do you do even if you lose a love one? Don't wait! Prepare yourself now by placing your faith in God! That faith will give you access to things such as strength, love, joy, peace, grace, patience, gratitude, wisdom, understanding and help in a time of need, and so on; all of which are available in Christ, and come from having faith in God through Christ. These are far greater treasures than anything (or anyone) tangible here on earth. Does it mean that you don't value the person if you're not devastated by their loss? Of course not! What it means is that you (with understanding) possess all the attributes of Christ, in greater value! Because of this you, by choice, refuse to allow even death to cause your stability in Christ to waver! Your strength, peace, joy; etc., remains fully intact and fully functional in the face of loss, and a help to those who share your loss.

Is it easy to be strong when you've lost a loved one? Absolutely not! Back in 1978 I was living a stable life in the United States Air Force, stationed at Homestead Air Force Base, Florida. My oldest brother, Ricky, was only twenty five years old; but had already lived a difficult and troubled life. Besides being very intelligent, and having a gentle and generous heart, Ricky had an entrepreneurial spirit; but he lacked the financial resources and family support to realise his dreams. Long story short; Ricky was unable to keep a job, he spent time in juvenile detention, and would often get into trouble when he drank too much alcohol. As a result, my mom and I thought it would be a good idea to ask Ricky if he would like to leave Philadelphia, and come to live with me in Florida, which he accepted. A few months after moving in with me, Ricky's body was found in a Florida canal. The police showed up at my door to give me the bad news, and I was beyond devastated! At that time I didn't know Jesus as I do now; neither did I have anyone in my life in Florida who did. It certainly would've helped, because death is hard on the living; it shouldn't be, if you're in Christ; but sadly, for some people, it is.

It's been many years since losing my brother Ricky, and now that I am in Christ, and I have understanding, I've made up my mind to never let death affect me the way Ricky's death did ever again; but instead, to be a pillar (with empathy) for those who have lost, and for those who share my loss. I've also lost an absentee father (whom I never knew); however, since losing my brother Ricky, I've lost my mother (Susie), two of my younger brothers (Johnny and Eric), my brother-in-law (Melvin - who was more in spirit like my biological brother), my father-in-law (Leon), all eight of my aunts and uncles, and shortly before completing this book, my mother-in-law (Ann). All of whom I was very close to and loved dearly, but I never shed a tear; instead, I've now allowed the Holy Spirit to have access to my life to the extent that I can be a rock and a comfort to those who grieve. Do I miss them? Absolutely! I believe however that I honour those I've lost far better by being a comfort to the living, to those they left behind, who now grieve; than I would by being devastated by their passing. My four children were encouraged (and perhaps a bit amazed) as they watched their dad glorify God, and give God praise, as I touched my mother's hand as she laid in her coffin. I demonstrated to them what was possible in the face of death when you're rooted in Christ. That most certainly blessed them, and changed their lives forever.

1 Corinthians 10:13 (KJV) "There hath no temptation taken you but such as is common to man: but God is faithful, who will not suffer you to be tempted above that ye are able; but will with the temptation also make a way to escape, that ye may be able to bear it."

1 Corinthians 10:14 (Amp) "Therefore, my dearly beloved, shun (keep clear away from, avoid by flight if need be) any sort of idolatry (of loving or venerating anything more than God)."

So what's in your "treasure chest"? Is it your family, or your friends, or your relationships, or your health, or your possessions, or your money, or your wealth; or is it all the attributes of Jesus by your faith in God through Christ? Attributes that cannot not spoil, be destroyed, or be stolen. What's in your "treasure chest"? Whatever it is; that's where your heart is, and if it's perishable, well...

What does all this have to do with managing your expectations? This chapter is about you managing your expectations instead of your expectations managing you. If you are managing your expectations; then you're seeking to understand, pursue, and fulfil what God wants for you; in all areas of your life, including your relationships, and in every situation and circumstance you face. You rejoice in good times, as well as in tribulations, and you do not allow your fallen nature (your flesh) to take away your gratitude, or hinder or distort God's desires for you and His peace in you. By contrast, if your expectations are managing you; then not only are you disquieted in trials, but you (in your flesh and in your own strength) pursue material things and relationships. Also, your peace of mind, joy and happiness are tied to those material things and relationships; therefore, if you should ever lose them, emotional devastation ensues.

So what does God want for you? God wants you to have everything you are purposed to have, which (according to Ephesians 3:20) is, "Above all you can ask or think"! God; however, doesn't want the pursuit of "things" to be your life's mission; instead, it is God's desire that you seek to understand the Kingdom of God and your place in it, and to seek God's righteousness, which we obtain by faith in our salvation through Jesus Christ (Mat 6:33).

Considering that God's desires for you are above all you could ask or even think, it makes absolute sense for you to trust God in this regard; rather than you trying to acquire stuff for yourself in your own strength, without God's help. So what does this mean? How do you allow God to give you that which He has purposed for you? By abandoning your flesh motivated desires, so that you're able to hear God's voice in any given situation. God never stops speaking to you, and He never stops showing you, so the less you are influenced by your flesh, the easier it will be for you to see and hear God in everything! You will know if you should make that call, you will know if you should say yes to that business deal, you will know if you should form an alliance with those individuals, you will know if you should marry and whom you should marry. You will see life's pitfalls, and thereby avoid becoming a victim. Your mind will be clear to form new ideas and create new inventions, you will know where to invest and how to invest; and in all of this, you will be honouring God with all that you acquire.

So seeking the kingdom of God and His righteousness is not about doing nothing except reading the bible and praying; you have to do something! God will order your steps (Psalms 37:23), but you have to be "stepping" to give God something to order!

Referring back to Philippians 4:11, above all, be content wherever you are in your journey of life; nonetheless, be aware that there is a very fine line between contentment and abandoned expectations. The question is, how can you

Managing Your Expectations

tell the difference? Actually, it's quite simple. If you say, or you feel that you are content, and in your state of contentment you have absolutely no thoughts of God's desire or ability to increase you in any way; then you are in a state of abandoned expectations. On the other hand, when you are truly content, your countenance (your attitude or emotional disposition) remains peaceful, no matter the circumstances; however, you always know with absolute certainty, that it is God's will that you are increased in every area of your life; spiritually and in the natural. Nonetheless, your only desire is to be led of the Holy Spirit as you pursue the will of God daily, in every situation, whatever that may entail; all the while knowing that by so doing, you will eventually fulfil God's purpose for your life. This is true contentment.

Please know that God's expectations for you are far greater than what you could possibly expect for yourself; but are never fulfilled by the pursuit of quantity of substance, but by quality of character. When you have great character, and you are yielded to the leading of the Holy Spirit, quantity of substance will take care of itself. In the end, when your brief time on earth has ended; not only would you have positively affected the lives of many by having accomplished great and meaningful things; but you get to go to heaven, and there, spend all eternity - the time that truly matters.

Under this new covenant (the covenant of grace) it's not a matter of being obedient to the old covenant Law in order to get stuff from God; it's a matter of being obedient to the leading of the Holy Spirit. In so doing, we will acquire in its entirety, all that God has already made available to us.

CHAPTER 12

The Language of Success

In this chapter, which is in some ways related to the previous chapter (Managing Your Expectations), I will address the profound effect what we speak can have on our lives.

Proverbs 18:21 (KJV) "Death and life are in the power of the tongue: and they that love it shall eat the fruit thereof." There are those who say a lot, and there are those who have a lot to say. "And they that love it..." is referring to people who love talking. Now I can talk the hind legs off a donkey, and as I continue to mature in Christ, it becomes increasingly important to me to be careful that what I say does not have an adverse effect on my life, or anyone else's. So you could say I love talking, because I do, not because I like talking just for the sake of running my mouth, but because I have a passion for speaking love and truth into people's lives; giving them encouragement, hope and purpose. By contrast, I'm not big on small talk, not at all, at some point the conversation must and always does evolve into weightier things.

"Death and life are in the power of the tongue…" What does that mean? It means that what you say will produce negative results or positive results, and not just on you; but on others if they are vulnerable. What do I mean by vulnerable? A child or even an adult who does not possess the spiritual wherewithal to protect themselves from carelessly spoken words that corrupt or destroy, rather than nurture or encourage. So if you love running your mouth, you may want to carefully consider your words to ensure that what you speak breathes life into situations and circumstances, and not death.

Ephesians 4:29 (KJV) "Let no corrupt communication proceed out of your mouth, but that which is good to the use of edifying, that it may minister grace unto the hearers." Let's get one thing straight here, "corrupt communication" does not mean profanity, or swearing, as some people call it. I don't swear, but I know some people who do, and some of them have more of the character and nature of Christ than some (so called) Christians I know! People who get hung up on other people swearing are completely missing the point. What do you think God judges, what comes out of your mouth, or what's in your heart? Your communication can be corrupt to it's core, laced with all kinds of evil, without using one swear word! On the other hand, I've heard people use all kinds of swear words to express positive and encouraging things about someone else. God sees the heart of a person. The "heart", meaning the deep inner core of the person, where their true nature resides; apart from that which is seen, or displayed on the surface, the innermost and true nature of the person; different to that which the person projects outwardly. So whether you swear or not, God sees and judges the heart of a person.

Now there is a case for not swearing, which is one of the reasons why I don't swear. **Romans 14:16 (KJV) "Let not then your good be evil spoken of."** I'm ex-military, United States Air Force, between 1977 and 1988. Back in those days, swearing was common place in the military, so I was "effin" and "jeffin" along with the best of them! Generally, swear words can be used to express a myriad of emotions, so after numerous years of swearing, I realised that I was unable to accurately express myself, or articulate my thoughts and emotions without using a swear word, and I thought to myself, "this is not good!". I wanted to be able to communicate more effectively, so using swear words in place of more descriptive, and accurate vocabulary, just wasn't cutting it.

Having surrendered my life to Christ and coming across Romans 14:16, I then had another reason to stop swearing. If for some people, swearing is perceived as corrupt communication; then personally, I do not want the name of Jesus to be associated with it. I am an ambassador for Christ; therefore, it is important for me to be sensitive to what may be a stumbling block for people, after all, Jesus died for them too, and loves them as much as He loves me, so I have an obligation to Jesus, to represent Him well in the presence of others. Not everyone is delivered from the bondages of religious laws and archaic doctrines of men so I take heed to Romans 14:16, and to what the Apostle Paul says in 1 Corinthians 6:12 (Amp) ***"Everything is permissible (allowable and lawful) for me; but not all things are helpful (good for me to do, expedient and profitable when considered with other things). Everything is lawful for me, but I will not become the slave of anything or be brought under its power."*** So I can swear if I want to, it won't affect my salvation, but it's not a practical or good thing for me to do when considered with other things. Okay, enough about swearing; I just needed to get that out of the way, but there is a deeper understanding of Proverbs 18:21 and Ephesians 4:29 that must be explored, so let's get on with it.

The Language of Success

Why is it that a person who sees themselves as good, and well grounded, will often say things that are unhelpful, or even destructive to or about someone, or (in many cases) to or about themselves? The reason is because our flesh is hardwired to fail! This is why there is a market for motivational speakers! All the motivational speaker does is help the listener to overcome their inherent nature to fail, or (at worse) self destruct. Failure and corruption is the default setting for the flesh so if you are not aware of this, you will without question be a party to corrupt communication, good person or not.

So how do you ensure that your words will always have pure intentions? This is where the Holy Spirit comes in. When you allow yourself to be filled with the genuine, unconditional, incorruptible love and glory of God, in the form of the Holy Spirit, and you measure your words by, and filter them through the Holy Spirit; you will find that your communication will always be appropriate for the occasion. You notice I said "appropriate" because if you are allowing the Holy Spirit to speak through you, there will be times when it is necessary for your words to be used in righteous indignation, for rebuke or correction, as Jesus did when He railed against the Scribes and Pharisees (Matthew 23:1-39), or when He said to Peter, "get thee behind me Satan" (Matthew 16:23 KJV). Nonetheless, Jesus' communications never came from a place of malice, or corruption; but from a place of love and authority, and if the hearers would heed to His words and repent, they would be better off for it.

So Godly communication may not always make you feel good, it all depends on how you receive it. Your responsibility as a Christian is to ensure that you recognise the difference between your flesh, and the Holy Spirit. You have to know the true redeeming, and grace filled nature of Jesus, a nature that is good and merciful, and a righteous defender and protector of the vulnerable; as well as judge, jury and executioner of all things evil. Your understanding and identification of the character and nature of Jesus Christ, combined with being surrendered to the leading of the Holy Spirit, will allow you to be consistent in your communication, in accordance with all scriptures relating to righteous communication.

Luke 6:45 (KJV) "A good man out of the good treasure of his heart bringeth forth that which is good; and an evil man out of the evil treasure of his heart bringeth forth that which is evil: for of the abundance of the heart his mouth speaketh."

No matter how you try to hide it, or fake it, eventually what's truly in your heart will come out of your mouth. So if you really want to be consistent in speaking truth, encouragement, and life; instead of condemnation and corruption, whether concerning yourself or someone else; then get filled with the righteousness of God, be led of the Holy Spirit, and your mouth will follow.

What you say you believe is not what you really believe, what you really believe is determined by what you do.

CHAPTER 13

Flesh and Spirit

What I'd like to explore here, is how to recognise your flesh (your fallen human nature), and how to recognise your spirit made righteous by God; or more specifically, the Holy Spirit within you. How do you identify or understand which is which? What should you do with that understanding? This subject is very important because if you're to be led by the Holy Spirit; you have to be able to recognise Him.

How many times have you heard people say; or seen people do something (supposedly) in the name of Jesus; but you know for sure that their words or actions are in conflict with the attributes of Jesus Christ? You be like, "I don't know what that is, but it sure ain't Jesus!"

Matthew 7:21-23 (KJV) [21] "Not every one that saith unto me, Lord, Lord, shall enter into the kingdom of heaven; but he that doeth the will of my Father which is in heaven. [22] Many will say to me in that day, Lord, Lord, have we not prophesied in thy name? and in thy name have cast out devils? and in thy name done many wonderful works? [23] And then will I profess unto them, I never knew you: depart from me, ye that work iniquity." These scriptures demonstrate the profound importance of knowing the voice of God; so that we can be certain that we are speaking, thinking; or behaving in accordance to His will.

We (the Christian) are no longer under the law; instead, we are led by the Holy Spirit; however, if we can't recognise His nature, if we can't recognise His voice; then how can we be led by Him? These are four questions I'd like to explore:

1. What would Jesus do? You can't answer that if you don't know the character of Christ.
2. What do we mean when we say "our flesh"?
3. How do we identify the character of Christ?
4. How does knowing the difference between the Holy Spirit and our flesh benefit us and others?

Flesh and Spirit

What would Jesus do? People sometimes ask this question playfully; however, it is the single most important question we must ask ourselves, if we truly desire to be led by the Holy Spirit. If we're to be led by the Holy Spirit, we must be able to recognise the Holy Spirit. What would Jesus do? Before we can truthfully answer this very important question, we must be careful with the assumptions we make about Jesus' nature or character.

For Jesus to be qualified to be an atonement for our sins, He Himself had to live a sinless life; so Jesus did not do the things we do to gratify our flesh. One small example: people say, "Jesus drank wine so he must've gotten drunk!" No, he would not have gotten drunk. Getting drunk is not something the Holy Spirit would lead Jesus; or any of us to do. For one, drunkenness weakens our inhibitions; making us more susceptible to our fallen nature; and two, Jesus was so aware of who He was (the Son of God), that doing things like getting drunk; or anything that represents gratification of the flesh, would have been far from Him. Some would say eating is gratifying the flesh. No. Eating food is a necessity to live; overeating is gratification of the flesh; but remember, the "flesh" is defined as human nature without God, which definitely does not apply to Jesus.

Should you then, feel condemned when your behaviour falls short of the righteousness of Jesus? Absolutely not! If you've accepted the salvation of God through Jesus Christ; then you are no longer condemned by your sinful nature, as far as God is concerned, you are righteous, period! Which means, you can die in a drunken stupor; and still go to heaven. This does not; however, mean that you shouldn't try to live according to your new righteous nature that God sees; but simply by virtue of being human, we will always fall short of the righteousness of God, no matter how good we think we are. Nonetheless, you should at least recognise and be honest about the things you do that are inconsistent with righteousness; otherwise, you will never be able to discern with certainty what is of God, and what is of your flesh; you just won't know the difference!

King David was repentant and honest before God about his fleshly weaknesses, and worshiped God all the more for it. Because of David's transparency before God; and because of his worshipful, repentant heart; God referred to David as the apple of His eye.

Many people do not know the true nature and character of Jesus Christ; however, it is the single most important question we should ask ourselves constantly as we go about our daily lives. What would Jesus do?

Romans 7:19 (KJV) "For the good that I would I do not: but the evil which I would not, that I do." Will you always do what you know Jesus would do in any given situation? No;

but if you're serious about being led by the Holy Spirit; then I encourage you to ask yourself, "is this what Jesus would think, say, or do in this situation?" In so doing, you will always be surrendered to the leading of the Holy Spirit; rather than fixated on doing your own thing regardless of whether it's consistent with the nature and character of Christ.

Still on the topic; "What would Jesus do?", when you watch television programs, watch movies, or listen to music; it's important to be aware of the effect it's having on you. I can testify that it's possible to watch programs with sexual content, violence and profanity; but be so astutely and consistently aware of the presence of the Holy Spirit; that I'm simply not affected by it. Sometimes however, protecting my heart and mind from the underlying spiritual corrosiveness of the content is too much hard work, so I listen to the Holy Spirit, and I switch it off.

Let's face it, we live in a fallen world, surrounded by corruption in all its forms; we mustn't be so fearful, so aloof, so disconnected that we're unable to discern what ails people; rendering us ineffective, and of no help to the broken and broken-hearted. Running around thinking we're "all that"; and telling people how bad they are, is not of Christ! We mustn't be so spiritually isolated that we have no idea what tools the devil uses via traditional media, or social media, or any other source to keep people enslaved by their flesh.

The same applies to the people you associate with, Christian or otherwise (I hope they're not all Christians!) Are they positively influenced by the spirit of grace and mercy that exudes from you; or are you negatively influenced by their fallen nature? Do you find yourself doing the things that they do that oppose the Holy Spirit? The Pharisees criticised Jesus for the company He kept, which were people considered by society to be "undesirables"; however, Jesus was never negatively influenced by them. Instead, He had a profound positive effect on their lives; and so should it be with you. There was a saying back in the day, "So spiritually minded, that you're no earthly good!" Don't be that person. Snobbery is not one of the characteristics of Jesus Christ.

1 Thessalonians 5:22 (KJV) "Abstain from all appearance of evil." Oh my goodness! Does this mean that Jesus was wrong for associating with people of "ill repute"?! Was Jesus wrong for allowing His disciples to pick corn (Matthew 12:1-8) on the sabbath day?! Absolutely not! You see my point? Those who have accepted Christ are no longer under the condemnation of the old covenant laws; but are in Christ, and under the new covenant of grace. You are exposed to corruption twenty four-seven, even in the form of your own flesh, which remains with you always, no matter how "good" you think you are; so it all depends on how you respond to this world and the people in it.

Identifying the areas in your life that you have not yet surrendered to God, that are not consistent with the attributes of Jesus Christ; requires constant awareness of God's presence. Is this possible? Absolutely! Not only is it possible; but because of the state of this fallen world, it's absolutely necessary! ***Matthew 24:24 (Amp) "For false Christs and false prophets will arise, and they will show great signs and wonders so as to deceive and lead astray, if possible, even the elect (God's chosen ones)."*** If it don't look like Jesus, if it don't walk like Jesus, if it don't talk like Jesus, it ain't Jesus; but how will you know if you don't know Jesus!? Oh I know you think you do; but do you? Really?!

So what do we mean when we say "our flesh"? Maybe I should've addressed this first in this chapter; but I can't be bothered to change it, so just roll with me. Anyhoooo... ***Romans 8:3 (Amp) "For God has done what the Law could not do, [its power] being weakened by the flesh (the entire nature of man without the Holy Spirit)."***

Our flesh is our human nature without the presence, leading and guidance of the Holy Spirit; in other words, our flesh is our fallen nature; the part of us which is not, and could never be surrendered to the Holy Spirit. Our flesh remains intact throughout our walk with Christ, it is never surrendered; but should be subdued.

Romans 8:1 (KJV) "There is therefore now no condemnation to them which are in Christ Jesus, who walk not after the

flesh, but after the Spirit." I often describe my flesh as nothing more than a passenger in my car, and not even in the front passenger seat; but in the back, or more often, in the trunk ("boot" if you're British); gagged and bound! My righteous nature has the wheel of this vehicle; but let's be real here; every now and again your flesh will try and grab the wheel, when it does, just slap it - Hard!

How do you identify the character and nature of Jesus Christ? There are many scriptures in the New Testament that will help you get to know Jesus, and I will suggest a few in a moment; in the meantime, what I believe defines Jesus' character more than anything is love. Not love as most people define love; where they will love you as long as you don't offend or hurt them, no; I'm talking about that all powerful true love, which is unconditional.

The unconditional love of Jesus gave Him not just the ability to see beyond the pretence of an individual; but the authority to speak truth to power with supernatural focus and spiritual precision; to the extent that though the recipients may outwardly reject Jesus' words, they could not dismiss the truth because of the conviction they felt in their hearts (Matthew 23:1-39). The unconditional love of Jesus, was the "force field" that protected (emotionally) His disciple Peter, when Jesus (of course looking directly at Peter) said, "Get behind me Satan"; but was actually speaking directly to the evil spirit behind what Peter had said to Him (Matthew 16:21-23). Jesus was not fearful of offending Peter because Jesus, God the Father, and the Holy Spirit knew that Peter knew undeniably that he was loved by Jesus. The unconditional love of Jesus allowed Him to see past the sin of a woman (John 8:1-12), and with one single sentence, convict a gathering of people prepared to stone her to death; and with another single sentence minister grace (unearned favour) to that same woman.

I really could go on and on about the power and authority of unconditional love, which so deeply characterises Jesus... so I will! Such is the unconditional love of Jesus that even His words of frustration (Matthew 17:17) were motivated by a deep, sincere and passionate desire to see all humanity walk in the power and the authority we once had, before the "fall". Such is the unconditional love of Jesus that even His fierce anger (Matthew 17:17) is without malice; but instead, a powerful display of righteous indignation. Such is the unconditional love of Jesus that though he was brutally beaten and nailed to a cross to die, slowly and painfully; He was able to speak these words (Luke 23:34), "Father forgive them, for they know not what they do."

These scripture references are just a few that I hope will help you better understand the character and nature of Jesus Christ. It's a really good start to build on; however, don't just read the scriptures, firstly, ask God to help you understand what you're reading; then meditate on it until you do.

The final thing I would suggest to you, concerning knowing the attributes of Christ, is that you pray without ceasing (1 Thessalonians 5:17). How does one pray without ceasing? By always being aware of the presence of God. How do you do that? By rejoicing and being grateful for all things, at all times and in every situation, good or (so called) bad.

Is this even possible?! Absolutely! The whole point of this chapter (and pretty much this whole book) is to help you identify the difference between your flesh, and your righteous spirit, which is in Christ; i.e, the Holy Spirit. When you're able to distinguish between the two, you then have the choice to obey or be influenced by one or the other.

Once you know someone, you can't "un-know" them, so when you know Christ, who actually lives in you; eventually the two of you become one and before you know it, your thoughts become His thoughts, and although these thoughts may be fully exposed to your flesh; you will always be aware of the presence of God, in spite of the decisions you make in the moment. Will you always obey the thoughts that you know are of God? No; however, this is what God has to say about that: **Romans 8:1 (KJV) "There is therefore now no condemnation to them which are in Christ Jesus, who walk not after the flesh, but after the Spirit."** Once you are in Christ, you are no longer led by the flesh; thereby, releasing you from the condemnation of the Law of the old covenant; you are instead led by the Holy Spirit. Please do not mistake this scripture as meaning: you're not condemned; as long as you don't do anything that may be of your flesh! It is impossible to be in Christ, and to be condemned at the same time! "Who walk not after the flesh, but after the Spirit." This is descriptive; in other words, it describes how a person in Christ is led (walks). If you are not in Christ, what or whom are you led by? Your flesh of course; which is subject to condemnation under the old covenant Law. Conversely, if you are in Christ, you are led by the Holy Spirit. Does this mean you will never be influenced by your flesh? Absolutely not, but you will not be condemned by it!

Believe it or not, I'm still talking about praying without ceasing! So what am I trying to get you to understand here? Condemnation causes you to feel guilty, causing you to focus on your flesh, your old sinful nature; instead of the Holy Spirit. If you are in Christ; then you are free from condemnation! You no longer have to allow the influences of your flesh to condemn you, or define who you are! The most important thing for you to glean from this is that how you define yourself (condemned or free from condemnation), will determine how you think, how you speak, and how you habitually behave. When you see yourself as God sees you (as the righteousness of God), your habits will change and you will be less influenced by your flesh and more influenced by the Holy Spirit. Just simply being in this state of mind causes you to be ever mindful of the presence of God; i.e., praying without ceasing.

You (the believer) are in Christ, and Christ is in you. Once you identify and understand the character and nature of Jesus; you will be able to say with honesty, and with certainty; that this thing that I'm feeling, thinking, saying, or doing; is of my flesh, and not of Christ.

How does knowing the difference between Spirit and flesh benefit you and others?

The more you become like Christ in your character, the more you surrender to and allow yourself to be influenced by the Holy Spirit; the greater your access to the supernatural things of the Kingdom of God, which includes greater understanding, spiritual wisdom, and power. Why is this a true statement? Because the very nature of sin is debilitating and destructive. So the more you identify with your flesh; instead of your righteous nature (which reflects the nature of Jesus), the more your fallen nature (your flesh) will be reflected in your life; rendering you proportionately ineffective in the power, purpose, and plans of God, and you're likely to be a detriment to yourself as well as a burden to others.

By contrast, the unconditional love (which is of Christ) and the power that accompanies it, will by default cause you to put the needs of others before yourself. It will give you the power to help people in ways you could never do in your flesh. Most importantly of all, you can't help someone out of a pit if you're in there with them! Yielding to the leading therefore of the Holy Spirit; instead of your flesh (because of your ability to differentiate between the two), will give you the ability to speak into the lives of others; removing the veil from their eyes, and like someone whose been taught to catch fish; instead of having fish given to them, will lead people to a self sustaining existence in Christ. The true and complete knowledge of who we are in Christ is all we need to be victorious in every aspect of our lives.

You may say, oh, I know a lot of people who don't profess to have Christ in their lives, and they're doing very well! Are they really? Have you examined their lives closely? And even if you have, and you believe that their lives are perfect in every way; the word of God says, "what does it profit a man to gain the world but lose his soul?!" Don't be deceived, the New Testament scriptures instructing us to be led of the Holy Spirit, instead of our flesh, are there for good reason. I've met a lot of people who do not profess to have Christ in their lives; however, they possess more of the attributes of Christ than some people who say they're in Christ! It's my personal belief that those people (the former) will at some point in their lives have an encounter with the Holy Spirit that will show them that He is the true source of their character; which I pray will persuade them to allow Christ into their lives, so that they may be complete in Him and that they may gain access to the Kingdom of God once their time has ended here on earth.

If we say we love God, and Jesus has saved us from death, and is the source of our strength and all that is good in our lives; then why wouldn't we want to be like him!? There are many scriptures that encourage you to be perfect, which means to acknowledge the fact that you have become reborn as a new creature, and that you are now in Christ who is perfect and complete; making you perfect and complete in Him. So you too become perfect by simple acknowledgement and acceptance of this truth.

I challenge you to examine your relationship with God. What is your motivation? Fear? Peer pressure? The desire to get wealth? Matthew 6:33 instructs us to seek first (which means as your one and only priority) the Kingdom of God and His righteousness, and (because God is good, and knows exactly what we have need of) all the good things you see other people enjoying shall be yours (emphasis on "good").

So when you say, "Jesus has delivered me from the curse of sin so I'm free and I can do whatever I like", that is accurate, you can do whatever you like. However, if doing whatever you like includes ignoring the leading of the Holy Spirit; then it will be reflected accordingly in your life. If you are choosing to be influenced by your flesh rather than the leading of Holy Spirit; you will fall short of experiencing the divine power and fulfilment God has preordained for you. You are in Christ, so you'll get to heaven; but if you ignore the leading of the Holy Spirit, how can you be led to the fulfilment of God's purpose for you here on earth?

One can have success without acknowledging God; however, it will be man's interpretation of success. God says, if you simply seek the Kingdom of God and His righteousness, you can have all the good things (emphasis on "good") other people desire, as well as the supernatural power available to you as the result of being surrendered to righteousness. It's not enough to just say I have been made righteous, you have to surrender to it as the Apostle Paul did. Paul recognised that he could do nothing about getting rid of his flesh, his sinful/fallen nature; however, what he could do was not allow himself to be habitually influenced by it; but rather, influenced by the leading of the Holy Spirit.

Jesus was so surrendered to righteousness that He was able to be the atonement for all of humanity! Within righteousness is the access to power, real power! Now you don't have to surrender to righteousness, you can just get by on

God's grace; however, who wants to be just getting by on grace when so much more is available to us by following God's instructions as written in the New Testament scriptures, and surrendering daily to the leading of the Holy Spirit.

Being led or influenced by your flesh, and doing whatever you want to do; rather than being influenced by your new righteous nature, and being led by the Holy Spirit, will hinder the purpose of God for your life. Don't get me wrong, you can get stuff, but it won't be God's stuff; you won't be walking in the power of God and experiencing the fullness of life you are (because of Jesus) entitled to.

If we're going to be followers of Jesus; then let's follow him. The key is to find your own personal reason why you should follow Jesus; then absolutely commit to it! Don't try, do! To "try" is to fail. To "do" is to succeed. The question you must ask yourself is, "do I want to be a trier or a doer?" You have nothing to lose, and everything to gain! Having said that; for those who are not in Christ, there is that one thing you can lose; what is it now...oh yeah; eternal life in heaven, yeah, you can lose that!

As I suggested before, your flesh is like a backseat driver; however, you (your righteous nature) have the wheel! What you need to say to your flesh is, "Flesh, you're a passenger, and I can't do anything about that; but I've got the wheel so sit there and be quiet!"

If you're believing for increase, do not allow thoughts about tomorrow to be based on where you are today.

CHAPTER 14

Fear - The Purpose Killer

After many years of trying, it was determined that Sarah, Abraham's wife was unable to have children. Such became Sarah's desperation, that she asked Abraham to have a child with her handmaid Hagar (Genesis 16). In spite of Sarah's inability to have children, God promised Abraham that he would have a son through her (Genesis 17). Years later, not only is Sarah still barren; but they're both past the physical ability to have children! So God waited until (in the natural) it was impossible for Abraham and Sarah to have children; then God says to Abraham, Sarah will have a son, and in spite of what Abraham could see in the natural, in spite of all logical human reasoning; Abraham believed God!

Now, Abraham and Sarah have a son whom they named Isaac, birthed from Sarah's womb; a son they'd waited many many years for, a son who was a miracle baby; a son whom Abraham and Sarah loved very very deeply, and what does God do? God commands Abraham to offer Isaac up as a sacrifice; in other words, kill him! What the heck!? But get this: not only does God want Isaac killed; He wants Abraham to do it! Double, "what-the-heck!!?" But, please see this very clearly, if Abraham was fearful of losing Isaac, if Abraham did not trust God enough to obey; we would not have the salvation we enjoy today. The only reason we can lay claim to heaven for us, for our children, for our grandchildren, and for all whom we love; is because Abraham was not fearful! The only reason God sacrificed His only Son Jesus, so that all of humanity could be redeemed, was because a human being was willing to sacrifice his only son first.

It was never God's intention for Abraham to kill Isaac; this was simply an exercise which allowed Abraham's faith to be activated causing God to react in kind.

God already knew Abraham wasn't fearful, God already knew that Abraham had faith; that's why He chose Abraham for this task in the first place! The only one who benefited from overcoming his fear was Abraham, and of course all of humanity! So like Abraham, overcoming fear not only benefits you; it benefits those whose lives you've been purposed to affect!

(Hebrews 10:1-18) God no longer requires a sacrifice from you as atonement for your sins; whether it be your possessions, houses, jobs, money, and most certainly not your children. What God requires of you is that you not be fearful of giving up or losing these things because fear blocks faith, and the absence of faith prevents God from doing for you all that He desires. God is the great provider; way beyond all you could ask or imagine. He is, and always will be great, and will forever desire the best for you, whether you believe it or not. Your faith or lack thereof neither increases, nor decreases God; however, it is in your best interest to have faith, for you and you alone (not God) will be the benefactor.

Just before Abraham struck Isaac with the knife, God stopped him, and provided him with a ram; whose horns were caught in a thick bush (Genesis 22:13). If the thought of leaving or losing your job, or not receiving income frightens you; then what does that say about your belief in the goodness, grace, mercy, and provision of God? Absolutely anyone who is walking in the power and purpose of God has had to overcome fear in some form or another! If just the thought of the Holy Spirit perhaps leading you to give up your source of income, or giving up anything that has become your source of comfort, causes you to be fearful; then you are not prepared to receive the mantle God has purposed for you.

The thing is, more often, what God requires of us more than anything (as he did with Abraham and Sarah), is that which we cherish the most, and with most people on the planet; what people cherish most (both for themselves and their loved ones), is comfort and security. There should be no other gods in our lives; however, with most people (without question), their god is some form of comfort and security, and the thought of losing it makes them fearful. Fear does not honour God. Fear gives power to Satan, and is a purpose killer!

Hebrews 13:5-6 (KJV) [5] "Let your conversation be without covetousness; and be content with such things as ye have: for He hath said, I will never leave thee, nor forsake thee. [6] So that we may boldly say, The Lord is my helper, and I will not fear what man shall do unto me." We overcome fear by believing God's Word which says, "I will never leave you or forsake you", and by remembering all the times God came through for us! So the answer isn't complicated; it's simple, as is everything with God. God is not evil; He does not make it impossible for you to walk in the fullness of His promises. That's why God abolished the law, because it was impossible for you to fulfil it; instead, God sent Jesus to fulfil the law on your behalf! Does that sound like a God who's making it so hard for you to receive His promises?! We ourselves complicate our lives and invite pain and suffering by not trusting God, and by not rejoicing and giving thanks during the trials of life, but instead choosing (in spite of all God has done for us) to be fearful.

2 Timothy 1:7 (KJV) "For God hath not given us the spirit of fear; but of power, and of love, and of a sound mind." God hasn't even given us the spirit of fear, so when we "choose" fear, that's on us!

Another way to overcome fear, is by weaning yourself off absorbing (or deliberately exposing yourself to) negative things that pull on your mind and your emotions in ways contrary to love, joy, happiness, and peace. So we (as the scriptures instruct) should think on these things... ***Philippians 4:8 (KJV) "Finally, brethren, whatsoever things are true, whatsoever things are honest, whatsoever things are just, whatsoever things are pure, whatsoever things are lovely, whatsoever things are of good report; if there be any virtue, and if there be any praise, think on these things."***

The instruction in God's Word; given to us that we may experience the Kingdom of God here on earth, and in the life hereafter; is what it is, and we simply shouldn't make excuses for our non-compliance. God will not change His Word to suit your lack of trust; and the acceptance of fear (concerning a thing, situation or circumstance), is the rejection of trust.

Having said all of that, please don't feel bad about being fearful regarding losing that which you cherish (for instance a child, family member, or loved one), as some things are just too big for us to carry; hence Abraham never told Sarah he was going away to "kill" Isaac as instructed by God; Sarah would've lost it! So Abraham told Sarah he was taking the boy to go worship God, and that they would return. God (and Abraham) knew that the boy was Sarah's weakness, so Abraham was wise not to tell her what God had commanded him to do.

It's not likely that you'll be able to hide your fears from your spouse or your partner, so what you must do at all costs, is make up your mind that you will not allow your fear to sabotage the purpose God has for your lives. Imagine if Abraham had told Sarah what God had commanded him to do with Isaac?! There would've been a battle up in that house! I can hear Sarah now: "You're gonna what?!!" No doubt, she would've likely talked Abraham out of it, or caused him to doubt, either way; bam! There goes our redemption!! If you struggle with fear, you mustn't give it fulfilment; i.e, give it life through your words or your actions, for in so doing; it will most definitely sabotage God's purpose and the provisions associated with God's purpose, which ultimately affects you and those around you.

Fearing your children, spouse, or partner might make wrong decisions must not be your motivation when praying. A prayer motivated by fear is not heard of God, but is an insult to His power. ***Hebrews 11:6 (KJV) "But without faith it is impossible to please Him: for he that cometh to God must believe that He is, and that He is a rewarder of them that diligently seek Him."*** God is not angry with you if you're fearful, if you lack faith. Like any good parent who wants what's best for you, God is the same in this regard; the difference is: God's desires for you far exceed that of any natural parent, so He is not pleased when your lack of faith prevents Him from providing for you that which He desires; i.e., answering your prayers (in accordance with His will of course). So don't misunderstand me here, it's okay to have fear come upon you; but when you pray, you must pray with faith, believing, and after you pray you should no longer "choose" to be fearful; otherwise again, you insult the goodness, grace, power, and majesty of God. So remember this when you pray. And afterwards, remember Philippians 4:8, "Think on these things…"

Do not be fearful in decision making. When two or more are involved, you should support each other's decisions with confidence in God, and confidence in each other's ability to hear His voice, and to order your steps. You should never throw fear motivated doubt into the situation by saying things like, "shouldn't you consider…" or "maybe we should...". If statements like that are motivated by fear; then they are destructive. If you do feel led to make statements like that; do so with certainty that what you're suggesting is through the leading of the Holy Spirit, which means it can be supported by the Word and the wisdom of God; which you must be able to articulate with revelation clarity for the sake of others involved; otherwise you've just thrown a "faith destroying grenade" into the situation! Fortunately, Sarah was completely unaware of what Abraham was up to, so "fear" was never given the opportunity to sabotage the salvation of all mankind.

It would be much easier if you just see each other, and all situations and circumstances, through the eyes of the Holy Spirit, so that you're always in agreement regarding all things. To be able to see yourself and others through the eyes of the Holy Spirit; it's crucial that you're able to tell the difference between the Holy Spirit and your flesh (which I pray this book will help you to do); but simply put, to know the Holy Spirit, you must read relevant scriptures and pray for understanding...Simples!

The fulfilment of God's purpose for you, and the person (or people) you're connected to, is in part dependent upon you not sabotaging one another (or yourself) through fear, or through any of the other spiritually debilitating emotions like; resentment, bitterness, and lack of forgiveness for example.   You; therefore, must stay vigilant regarding your thoughts, and the motivations and meditations of your heart. Let your thoughts and the meditation of your heart be of good things; what God expects for you, which is good, and not evil (Jeremiah 29:11). Guard your heart; therefore, in this matter, for out of the abundance of your heart, your mouth will speak (Luke 6:45), and because of fear; the purpose of God for you in that moment, or at worst, for your life, can be sabotaged just by what you speak.

*There's no such thing as a 'bad day';
it all depends on how you respond
to the events therein.*

CHAPTER 15

My Flesh is Not My Friend!

Firstly, let's identify the issue you must overcome. The issue isn't your flesh of itself; let's face it, our flesh isn't going anywhere. The issue, or problem is allowing yourself to be influenced by your flesh; i.e., when you allow your flesh to run rampant, unchecked, and you make excuses for your flesh; instead of seeing it for the destructive force that it is.

Let's recap. What is our flesh? Our flesh is defined as: human nature without the presence of (or relationship with) God.

My Flesh is Not My Friend!

Romans 7:24 (KJV) "O wretched man that I am! Who shall deliver me from the body of this death?!" Paul despised his flesh, and rightly so, because our flesh is opposed to God, and all things righteous. *Galatians 5:17 (Amp) "For the desires of the flesh are opposed to the Holy Spirit, and the desires of the Spirit are opposed to the flesh (godless human nature); for these are antagonistic to each other, continually withstanding and in conflict with each other, so that you are not free but are prevented from doing what you desire to do."* Look at what the Apostle Paul says in *Romans 7:19-20 (AMP) [19] "For I fail to practice the good deeds I desire to do, but the evil deeds that I do not desire to do are what I am ever doing." [20] "Now if I do what I do not desire to do, it is no longer I doing it, it is not myself that acts, but the sin principle which dwells within me fixed and operating in my soul."* Paul is talking about his flesh! This is why Paul exclaimed, "O wretched man that I am!" Paul; however, went on to say that Jesus would deliver him: *Romans 7:25 (AMP) "O thank God! He will! through Jesus Christ (the Anointed One) our Lord! So then indeed I, of myself with the mind and heart, serve the Law of God, but with the flesh the law of sin."*

You don't offer shelter, protection, or excuses for an enemy who wishes to harm you, so why make excuses for your flesh?! If the great Apostle Paul is humble, honest, and clear-minded enough to call his flesh out; then how much more us!

Righteous indignation, and renewed determination to be led of the Holy Spirit, and to do good in the sight of God; should be our state of mind whenever we fall foul to the influences of our flesh.

As Christians, having been set free from condemnation of the Law; we are now led by the Holy Spirit. Our greatest challenge; however, is to be able to differentiate between the Holy Spirit, who speaks to us through our renewed righteous spirit; and our flesh, which opposes God. How can you tell if what you're thinking, saying, or doing is of the nature, and character of Jesus Christ or of your flesh; your fallen nature. This is the big question, and I hope to answer it in this chapter.

Jeremiah 29:11 (KJV) ***"For I know the thoughts that I think toward you, saith the Lord, thoughts of peace, and not of evil, to give you an expected end."*** God desires to give us an expected end; in other words, a meaningful and fulfilling life; however, whether that is achieved or not depends on how much we allow ourselves to be led of the Holy Spirit. Sadly, it's difficult for many people to consistently surrender to the leading of the Holy Spirit; being hindered by their own unwillingness to see their flesh as their enemy. No one wants to see themselves as a bad person, and that, right there, is the problem! The reality is, from God's perspective we are all bad people! The old covenant Law proves it; our inability to keep the Law exposes the corrupt nature of humanity.

My Flesh is Not My Friend!

The requirement of the commandments (The Laws), was that we must obey not just the famous Ten Commandments, but without exception or error; every single one of them (all 613), and to break one of them made us guilty as if we'd broken them all! ***James 2:10 (Amp) "For whosoever keeps the Law as a whole but stumbles and offends in one single instance has become guilty of breaking all of it."*** Sounds harsh doesn't it? No! Why? Because God never intended for us to obey these laws in the first place; He knew we couldn't! Galatians 3:13 explains that the law was a curse upon us because no one could fulfil it!

Okay, you're probably freaking out about now thinking, "well what the heck was point of all these laws then?!" Let me explain: Because of Abraham's faithfulness, God promised Abraham that through his Seed (Jesus Christ); all of humanity would be saved from the curse of the law if we (like Abraham believed God) believe in our salvation through Jesus, by faith. There were no laws for Abraham to obey to make him righteous before God; however, such was the greatness of Abraham's faith in God, that God credited Abraham's faith as righteousness (Gen 15:6 and Rom 4:3).

So what, or shall I say, whom should we have faith in? Jesus Christ! That He paid the price for our redemption; making us (by faith) righteous before God. Yes, I know; I still haven't explained the purpose of the law; keep your pants on! This scripture explains it clearly: ***Galatians 3:19 (Amp) "What then was the purpose of the Law? It was added [later on, after the promise, to disclose and expose to men their guilt] because of transgressions and [to make men more conscious of the sinfulness] of sin; and it was intended to be in effect until the Seed (the Descendant, the Heir) should come, to and concerning Whom the promise had been made. And it [the Law] was arranged and ordained and appointed through the instrumentality of angels [and was given] by the hand (in the person) of a go-between [Moses, an intermediary person between God and man]."*** Okay, yeah it's wordy, so simply put; God is saying to humanity through the law, "Uh y'all ain't all that; y'all need a saviour!" So from God's perspective, there are no good people, we are all corrupted and in need of a redeemer, so that He can again see us as righteous, as it was before the fall of humanity.

Bottom line? Our flesh is in opposition with God, and for this reason we need to see our fallen nature (our flesh) for what it is; stop protecting it, and call it out! None of us wants to fight against God; we've invited Him into our lives to operate freely, so we have no (intentional) desire to fight against God. My desire in this chapter, is to show you (with the help of the Holy Spirit and the scriptures) that your flesh is your enemy, and not just your enemy, but also the enemy of God. Your flesh will undermine every good thing God has for you because it is hostile towards God.

My Flesh is Not My Friend!

How do we overcome the destructive nature of our flesh? Let's look at it in four parts:

1. Things We Take For Granted
2. Sabotage
3. Becoming Aware
4. Staying Aware

Things we take for granted is where it all begins. Not being aware of what we're thinking about, or the effect our thoughts have on us or on others in any given moment, or situation; is a road that leads to pain, suffering, lack, loss, and unfulfilled dreams (yours and possibly the dreams of others). The measure by which you experience the power of God working in your lives will be determined by which nature you feed, what you feed it, and how much of it you consume. What do you feed more, your fallen nature (your flesh) or your renewed spirit, made righteous in Christ? Garbage in, garbage out! Holy Spirit in; power, honour, favour, joy, peace, love, strength, wisdom, understanding out! The latter sounds like good value to me!

There are many ways you can "feed" yourself (negatively or positively); however, primarily it's by what you consume through your eyes, your ears, or through people or things you associate with. The things you consume, or the people, or things you associate with are not of themselves (in isolation) the issue; it's your thoughts in relationship to these things. What do I mean by this? (Just thought I'd jump in here before you asked.) What I mean is how we respond emotionally or in our thinking to the things we observe with our eyes, things we hear, and the people or things we identify with; will determine whether we are feeding our flesh, or our renewed nature in Christ.

Let's think of the nature of Christ that dwells within the Christian as a variety of seeds. If the person truly is in Christ, and not just Christian by title - you shall know them by their fruit - (Matthew 7:15-20). There will be seeds of love, joy, patience, peace, gratitude, forgiveness, self control, self confidence, self esteem; seeds of grace and so on, and so on. Just a note here to say that it's important to be aware of all the seeds that make up the nature of Christ, so that we may remain alert to protect them.

Now let's take one seed; grace for instance (grace is defined as unearned/unmerited favour or unearned forgiveness), and let's say you're watching a movie and a person is expressing hatred and rage because someone has wronged them in some way (it could be anything). The moment you identify with that hatred and rage, the moment you take on board those emotions by imagining yourself in their position, or that situation; possibly thinking, or saying something like, "If I were them, I would kill that person!" Bam! You've just lost the seed of grace! It's gone! It's not suddenly going to come back at another time when it's required. Why? Because the moment you surrender to the seed of rage and un-forgiveness from your flesh; your flesh opposes the seed of grace, and the two cannot be in operation at the same time.

So what happened there? Why did you lose the seed of grace in that situation? Because of lack of understanding. ***Matthew 13:19 (KJV) "When any one heareth the word of the kingdom, and understandeth it not, then cometh the wicked one, and catcheth away that which was sown in his heart. This is he which received seed by the way side."*** Surely (you say) we can be vengeful one moment, and full of grace the next; can't we?! Yes, you can behave that way; however, that's exactly how our flesh behaves, and it's counterfeit! Anyone can say, or even perform like they understand the Word of the Kingdom of God; however eventually they will be caught off guard, and their true nature will be exposed. Why? Because our flesh opposes the things of God, and is self destructive by default!

In this example, a person says or thinks they understand grace; however when grace is required it isn't available because, having heard about grace, they never understood grace; therefore, the seed of grace was stolen from them. The sad thing is, many people don't even realise they're missing the seeds of the Kingdom of God until it's required, but unavailable.

Can we get the seed back? Absolutely! ***Matthew 13:11-12 (KJV) [11] "He answered and said unto them, Because it is given unto you to know the mysteries of the kingdom of heaven, but to them it is not given. [12] For whosoever hath, to him shall be given, and he shall have more abundance: but whosoever hath not, from him shall be taken away even that he hath."*** "To them it is **given**..." It is God that gives us the ability to understand the mysteries of the Kingdom of God (the Word of God)! Have you asked? Really? Sincerely? Simply (with sincerity) ask the Holy Spirit for understanding of the scriptures (the Word of God); then meditate on it until you do! How will you know when you have it? How will you know when you really do understand? When a situation arises, and what you say or think you understand is actually applied in that situation! The good news is, once you understand it, you will never "not" understand it!

So what should you do when you're watching a program that contains violence, or sexual content, or anything designed to appeal to your fallen nature? Be aware of how it's making you feel, because if you're not aware; then "seeds" could be being stolen from you left, right, and centre, and you'd be totally oblivious to it! If you're aware of how it's making you feel; then you're able to make the judgement whether to continue watching it, or to switch it off.

Now what I'm about to say here is of particular importance, because there are so many misguided Christians (in particular) who fall into this trap: Concerning the programs, or movies you watch; Do not be led by guilt, shame, or even by how you (or other people) think you should behave because you're a Christian; instead, be led by the Holy Spirit!

If you truly are solid in your understanding concerning the "seeds" that make you righteous in Christ; then the stuff you watch will not affect you! Be led of the Holy Spirit, because He just might want you to watch it; just so that you can see the abstruse insidiousness of the devil's activities against the conscience of humanity. Eventually, over time, fewer and fewer of the things you used to watch will continue to appeal to you; because you will find absolutely no value in watching them. You won't be pridefully thinking, "Oh, look at me; I'm so righteous", or trying to impress your friends, or even trying to impress God, for He knows what's really in your heart anyway! You instead, just won't want to watch it; because it simply no longer appeals to you.

So just to be clear, the seed of grace which I'm using in my example still remains within the Holy Spirit who dwells in you, however because of lack of understanding; access to the "seed" is lost, or stolen in the moment when you align yourself emotionally (in this example) with rage and un-forgiveness.

The Holy Spirit dwells in all who invite him in, however our ability to walk in our new righteous nature is wholly determined by how much we align our thoughts and behaviour with the personality and character of Jesus through understanding. How do we get to know the character of Jesus? Just ask God for understanding. Talk to Him! Ask God to reveal to you the true character and personality of Jesus. Also, read the scriptures about Jesus, and meditate on them; in particular, the ones where Jesus Himself is speaking. Endeavour to understand the character of someone who, being the personification of righteousness, allowed Himself to take the blame for the corrupted nature of all humanity; forgiving us, redeeming us, and restoring to us eternal life. That's a very special person, and God encourages us to be just like Him in our character; however, our flesh, our fallen human nature, will continue to hinder us if we don't recognise it's self destructive nature and keep it under subjection. My flesh is not my friend!

So Jesus talks about "seed" being lost or stolen in the parable of the sower in Matthew, chapter 13, as I've mentioned earlier. Jesus is referring to the Word of the kingdom of God as "seed". When you've been given the Word of God (again, in this example) concerning grace and forgiveness, and you truly understand it, it will be activated in every situation that requires it. If you truly possess and understand it; it will be functional in every situation or circumstance that requires it, plain and simple. If you have it, you have it! It's not simply the knowledge of grace that you have, but the understanding of it. Therefore, it is impossible for it not to operate through you, because when you understand a Godly principal or characteristic, it becomes a part of who you are.

I enjoyed eight years as medical sales rep. Once I understood a particular medical device (a medical implant for instance), which of course included it's function and purpose, along with understanding the surgical technique; there was never a time where I could not properly instruct the surgeon during surgery; guiding him or her through the surgical technique. There was never a situation where I didn't apply what I understood. What I understood about the product and the surgical technique became a part of who I was as a medical rep, so there was never a situation where I didn't use this understanding when it was required. It was impossible for me not to! The same goes for understanding the knowledge of the kingdom of God!

Once you have understanding of a Godly principal or truth (and I mean understand it, not just hear it) it will forever function in your life. Even though our flesh constantly opposes our Godly nature; a person who understands a

Godly principal or truth, will always overcome their flesh in that area.

I challenge you to name one good thing your fallen nature has accomplished for you! Not "good" in your opinion, but something God would consider good. Again, still on my grace example: If you do not understand grace, and you allow the "seed" to be stolen from you as the result of your reaction to something you exposed yourself to; you may "think" that you still possess the seed of grace. However, I guarantee you that because of the destructive nature of your flesh, the desire for vengeance will show up again, in a different scenario, and most likely just when it can do the most damage to the promises and purpose of God for you in that moment, and that moment could be the moment you were meant to see the manifestation of a blessing from God. Poof; blessing gone! Extending grace in one instance, and not in another, is nothing more than the flesh producing a counterfeit version of grace, it's fraudulent! Oh yes, we know how to perform, no one likes to think of themselves as a bad person, but just like counterfeit money, it's only a matter of time before it's exposed as a fake! The truth of the matter is, our flesh is what caused Jesus to be brutally beaten and nailed to a cross to die a slow and painful death! So why do we make excuses for it?!! The great Apostle Paul most certainly

My Flesh is Not My Friend!

didn't: ***"O wretched man that I am! Who shall deliver me from the body of this death?"*** (Romans 7:24 KJV)

Speaking of grace - this gospel of grace is wonderful; however, know this, that the fulfilment of the purpose and promises of God for and in your life is not dependent upon grace alone, but on your cooperation with the Holy Spirit! In other words, we can't just say, think or do whatever we like and think that the grace of God will cause the abundance of blessings to flow into our lives. Oh you'll have stuff, but the "abundance" (spiritual and natural) that God has purposed for you will only be experienced by the daily subduing of your flesh and allowing yourself to be influenced by, and led of, the Holy Spirit. If it's good for us to live a "devil may care - do whatever we like" life, and still see the fulfilment of God's purpose; then what are the New Testament scriptures concerning our lives in Christ for? What are they all about?!

Grace is the gift that is responsible for our salvation. Grace is available to us because without it we will not see the Kingdom of God when our life leaves our body, no matter how "good" we think we are. Grace is not a free pass to the abundance of God's blessings regardless of how we think, act or speak! If we don't protect our righteous nature in Christ from our fallen nature (our flesh); then we will fall short of the fullness of blessings God desires for us here on earth. Oh we'll get to heaven alright (grace will see to that), but we'll go there broke, busted and disgusted! Don't get me wrong; we all can acquire stuff, we all can accumulate wealth in our own strength and efforts without God; however, it won't be the stuff God has purposed for us, and God says in **Mark 8:36 (Amp)**

"For what does it profit a man to gain the whole world, and forfeit his life in the eternal kingdom of God?" My flesh is not my friend!

So what do people take for granted. One thing for sure is that they assume they can identify with, associate with, watch, say, think, or do things that are inconsistent with righteousness; without there being any negative consequences. As I said: garbage in, garbage out! What's the solution? No matter what you're watching, what you're doing, who you're with, what you're saying or what you're thinking; never lose awareness of the presence of the Holy Spirit. It's that simple! If you acknowledge Him, the Holy Spirit will constantly speak to you in the situation, or in the moment. Also, spend more time reading scriptures about who you are in Christ, and how to project His righteousness outwardly, in your daily life.

I've watched programs or movies with profanity, sex and violence in them, and have gotten material for my sermons! Why? For one: I'm constantly aware of the presence of the Holy Spirit, I never switch Him off, so He speaks to

My Flesh is Not My Friend!

me constantly, irregardless of what I'm doing. Secondly: I am astutely aware of how I'm reacting to what I'm hearing or seeing; therefore, I'm consciously protecting myself from becoming a victim of stolen "seeds". Now by contrast, I've watched some stuff for five minutes, and found it too exhausting to try and protect the seeds (my understanding of the Word of God) within me! So, because I'm constantly aware of the presence of the Holy Spirit, I can tell within minutes that the intent of the program is completely insidious; created with no other intention, other than to deliberately appeal to absolutely nothing but the fallen nature in me, so "Click"; I switch it off! The question we must ask ourselves is, what do we identify as "entertainment"?

Now, if you're switching something off because of guilt; then don't bother. Guilt does not set you free. Understanding truth is what sets you free! Guilt just keeps you in bondage, which then makes you feel bad, so you end up pleasing your flesh in other ways so that you can feel good again; only to feel even guiltier! Can you see subtle deceptiveness of it all?! Therefore, if you're going to switch something off, switch it off because you understand **why** you should; but not because of guilt! However, be encouraged, for as you journey to understand; God's grace will keep you, because what God desires for you to experience concerning your flesh is not condemnation and guilt, but righteous indignation. Remember, your flesh is hostile towards God. Righteous indignation against your flesh, and determination to be influenced by the Holy Spirit should be your state of mind when you fall foul to the influences of your flesh. You should be like, "There's no way I'm gonna allow my flesh to insult the grace of God and sabotage the life God desires for me!" Which, by the way, is the perfect segue to my next point: Sabotage!

For the Christian, the measure of success you experience in life will be determined by whether you are influenced by the Holy Spirit or your flesh; however, do not confuse "success" with the amount of money you make, or the stuff you accumulate (please remember Mark 8:36). God has a whole bunch of "stuff" for us; however, He says, instead of desiring after it; seek the Kingdom of God and His righteousness, and "stuff" will be added to us via His will; rather than via the workings of our flesh. Why (I hear you ask) does God ask us to prioritise our lives in this way? Because in so doing, when we receive earthly possessions from God, they don't end up becoming the object of worship, or the source of our strength, and our joy, for if they do; they can become the things that destroy us if we should lose them, but that's a whole other conversation.

Back to sabotage. It astonishes me when I think about the things we do impulsively; without thinking about whether it's of the Holy Spirit, or our flesh; as a result, we sabotage the purpose of God for ourselves in the moment, situation, or at worse for a lifetime.

"Sabotage" is called such, because it is a destructive or disruptive action or event that exists without you being aware of it. Sabotage (spiritually speaking) catches you unaware with the intention of incapacitating you, or at worst, destroying you spiritually or physically, or both!

So what am I talking about here? How do you recognise and avoid those things you say, think or do that sabotages your life? The answer is, by knowing the nature of Jesus and allowing His nature to become your nature. Now I can only give you the ladder to get over the wall, but it's up to you to do the climbing, and there most certainly is some climbing involved if you are to know the nature of Jesus to the extent that your thoughts, actions and words become the spiritual conduits through which the blessings of God flow instead of conduits through which flow destruction.

Moving on: We're still talking about recognising that your flesh is not your friend. What do you have to do to become "woke"? For starters, honesty is the road to deliverance. You must accept that the New Testament scriptures given to us under the new covenant of grace are there for a reason; not to condemn us (absolutely not), but to help us fight back against the influences of our flesh, and to overcome the barrage of evil and temptations we face every single day in this fallen world.

In this fallen world; you are bombarded every day with stuff that is designed to kill, steal, or destroy the fullness of life God desires for you. Just look around you; it's in the news, in tv commercials, it's in the conversations people have with you (even the ones who say they're Christian), and it's absolutely rampant in social media. In fact, social media is the most effective tool used by the devil. Why? Because it offers the greatest concentration of brokenness and fallen humanity, even in those posts that seem innocent; all in one neat platform. All you have to do is be exposed to a post, Tweet, or image long enough to allow your flesh to influence your thoughts, emotion, or opinion and bam; a "seed" is stolen!

Let me take a moment to remind you that you have protection against the pitfalls of social media. Stay spiritually alert! All you have to do is recognise what happened in the moment. You must recognise that your thoughts, words or actions caused a particular seed to attempt to be stolen, so you reject it: ***2 Corinthians 10:5 (KJV) "Casting down imaginations, and every high thing that exalteth itself against the knowledge of God, and bringing into captivity every thought to the obedience of Christ."*** You make up your mind that this attempt (by this particular thing, in this situation) to steal your "seed"; will never happen again, and you speak out against what just occurred; declaring in the name of Jesus that you are the righteousness of God! Now here's the thing, the devil doesn't care how many times you speak against him, as long as you keep falling in that area; over and over again! You get the seed, you don't understand it, you lose the seed, you get the seed, you don't understand it, you lose the seed; over, and over again. So you end up going absolutely nowhere which, in many ways, is similar to defeat. Who wants to live like that?!

So how do you become aware ("woke")? By being honest about your own fallen nature and stop making excuses for it! Also, by recognising that we live in a fallen world, with evil woven into the very fabric of it; so much so, that people see the byproduct of evil such as poverty, hate, lust, lack of self control, despair, earthly desires, greed, insecurity, pride, boastfulness, anger, condemnation, and so forth; existing alongside goodness, peace, and all things righteous, so people feel it's normal to live a life where both good and evil have equal footing in their lives. Your flesh should not have equal footing in your life along with your righteous nature. Your flesh will be with you always as you journey through life; however, it should be nothing more than a passenger, and if possible, have no influence on you whatsoever.

Now that you're "woke", how do you stay woke? It's simply love that keeps you woke. Why? ***1 Peter 4:8 (Amp) "Above all things have intense and unfailing love for one another, for love covers a multitude of sins <u>forgives and disregards the offences</u>***

of others." It's one thing to be told you're not condemned; it's another not to feel condemned, and it's even another to be able to explain why you're not and don't feel condemned. I have not rejected God, and He has not abandoned me to my own fleshly desires; therefore, I can laugh at the jokes of comedians who use profanity because of love; i.e., I forgive and disregard the offences of the flesh, be it my own or someone else's.

I am forever mindful of the significance of not becoming offended by the behaviour of others, for I too am subject to a fallen nature, and though I may not commit the same offence as my neighbour, I nonetheless do commit offences, and in the eyes of God they are all the same, so I do not judge. As the scriptures says, "He that is without sin among you, let him first cast a stone at her." (John 8:7)

Thanks be to God for His grace and for the leading of the Holy Spirit, because I know my flesh is not my friend, and by God's grace and the leading of the Holy Spirit; you too can remain forever woke regarding this.

Corruption is like nuclear waste; if you handle it, eventually it will not only harm you, but the people close to you as well.

CHAPTER 16

A Message to the Self-Righteous

Get a life! Just kidding...but get a life!

What I've witnessed in some churches in the past and even in the present, is the practice of preaching the gospel of Jesus Christ (which is a gospel of grace and forgiveness) as laws to be obeyed; otherwise, suffer punishment. The New Testament scriptures specifically relating to our behaviour, are not laws (the Law was fulfilled in Christ), and they are not commandments; except for this one exception: ***John 13:34-35 (KJV) [34] "A new commandment I give unto***

A Message to the Self-Righteous

you, That ye love one another; as I have loved you, that ye also love one another. [35] By this shall all men know that ye are my disciples, if ye have love one to another." Other than this beautiful commandment; the New Testament scriptures relating to behaviour are simply instructions on how we should conduct ourselves, so that our flesh doesn't hinder us from experiencing the abundant life here on earth that God desires for us.

When the gospel is preached as if it were something to obey; otherwise, suffer punishment as in the old days before the Law was fulfilled in Christ; then we insult Jesus' crucifixion on the cross; suggesting we have to "behave" our way into heaven. Paul makes this very, very clear in Galatians chapter 3 (I encourage you to read it); in the meantime, these scriptures in particular sum it up: *Galatians 3:1-3 (Amp) [1] "O You poor and silly and thoughtless and unreflecting and senseless Galatians! Who has fascinated or bewitched or cast a spell over you, unto whom--right before your very eyes--Jesus Christ (the Messiah) was openly and graphically set forth and portrayed as crucified? [2] Let me ask you this one question: Did you receive the Holy Spirit as the result of obeying the Law and doing its works, or was it by hearing the message of the Gospel and believing it? Was it from observing a law of rituals or from a message of faith? [3] Are you so foolish and so senseless and so silly? Having begun your new life spiritually* with the Holy Spirit, are you now reaching perfection by dependence on the flesh?"

John 8:10-11 (KJV) [10] "When Jesus had lifted up himself, and saw none but the woman, He said unto her, Woman, where are those thine accusers? hath no man condemned thee? [11] She said, No man, Lord. And Jesus said unto her, Neither do I condemn thee: go, and sin no more." The scriptures of John 8:1-11, characterise the heart of God towards humanity regarding sin, more than any other. And don't go trying to separate the nature and character of Jesus, from the nature and character of God! ***John 14:9 (Amp) "Jesus replied, Have I been with all of you for so long a time, and do you not recognise and know Me yet, Philip? Anyone who has seen Me has seen the Father. How can you say then, show us the Father?"***

"Sinful" is the word used to describe the fallen nature of all of humanity. None of us are immune to or excluded from this fallen nature; not even those of us who accept salvation through Jesus Christ. Yes, the Christian has been given a new nature in Christ, but our old sinful nature still remains present with us, like smoke residue from a fire. The Apostle Paul put it this way: ***Romans 7:19-25 (Amp)***

[19] "For I fail to practice the good deeds I desire to do, but the evil deeds that I do not desire to do are what I am ever doing. [20] Now if I do what I do not desire to do, it is no longer I doing it it is not myself that acts, but the sin principle which

A Message to the Self-Righteous

dwells within me fixed and operating in my soul. [21] So I find it to be a law (rule of action of my being) that when I want to do what is right and good, evil is ever present with me and I am subject to its insistent demands. [22] For I endorse and delight in the Law of God in my inmost self with my new nature. [23] But I discern in my bodily members in the sensitive appetites and wills of the flesh a different law (rule of action) at war against the law of my mind (my reason) and making me a prisoner to the law of sin that dwells in my bodily organs in the sensitive appetites and wills of the flesh. [24] O unhappy and pitiable and wretched man that I am! Who will release and deliver me from the shackles of this body of death? [25] O thank God! He will! through Jesus Christ (the Anointed One) our Lord! So then indeed I, of myself with the mind and heart, serve the Law of God, but with the flesh the law of sin."

Our sinful nature does not make us God's enemy, no more than the woman in John 8:1-11 to whom Jesus said, "Neither do I condemn you", and sent her away with the instruction to sin no more. Now some people would say, Jesus commanded her to sin no more! First of all, it was not a commandment, it was an instruction, and secondly, Jesus didn't say "sin no more or else!" The sins of humanity (our fallen nature) neither increase, nor decrease God; God is sovereign, and doesn't need our assistance to be great! God's response to our fallen nature is and always will be compassion!

If Jesus didn't condemn the woman for her sin; then why did He say to her, "sin no more"? The answer is: God clearly isn't even remotely affected by our sin; we are! The choices we make in life, both spiritual, and in the natural; will determine the quality of life we'll enjoy, and please don't mistake quality with quantity. You can have stuff and be more broken, corrupted, and destitute than a person who has nothing; but is full of the character, love and compassion of Christ, and by the way; you don't have to be a Christian to have these qualities. Note: If you aren't a Christian, and you have these qualities, you may want to go ahead and get your ticket to heaven by simply accepting your salvation through Jesus Christ. But, back to my point. Who made you (the self righteous) the sin police?!

If you profess to be a Christian (or otherwise), and this chapter is making you angry, because you want to see everyone burn in hell who isn't just like you; then my heart breaks for you, because you share the same place in God's eyes as the Scribes and Pharisees that Jesus railed against because they kept people (whom Jesus came to set free) in fear and in spiritual bondage! You may think you have good intentions; however, the reality is, you just can't shake off the echos of the "thou shall not" Old Testament Laws, which reverberate in the hearts and minds of many people (especially the self-righteous), because vengeance and punishment appeals to humanity's fallen nature.

A Message to the Self-Righteous

Matthew 7:22-23 (KJV) [22] Many will say to me in that day, Lord, Lord, have we not prophesied in thy name? And in thy name have cast out devils? And in thy name done many wonderful works?

[23] And then will I profess unto them, I never knew you: depart from me, ye that work iniquity." Why would Jesus say to this to these people, who would've professed to be Christians, and would've apparently done all these good things? "Workers of evil"?! The answer is simple: these people are motivated by their flesh, and not by the leading of the Holy Spirit. Their actions absolutely, and without question, could not have been influenced by the Holy Spirit; otherwise Jesus would not reject them!

How does one get caught up thinking they're doing good, only to find out in the end that what they were doing was never of God? How can the person tell, so that they don't end up with "holy egg" on their face in the end? Well ask yourself, is what I'm saying or doing helping people (non-believers in particular) to feel loved? Do I help them to feel forgiven? Do I help them to feel like they've been set free? Does what I say or do make them want to run to Jesus, because they feel delivered from condemnation? Or do you make people who are lost (people for whom Jesus was crucified to save) feel guilty, and sorry, and fearful, and you insist that they ask God for forgiveness, for fear of going to hell?

So, what you're saying is: you want to shame and frighten people into loving God. Really?! You think people should love God out of fear of being punished?! Can you not see the contradiction in this? That's like someone saying, "My father would threaten to beat me, hurt my mother and destroy everything in our lives, so we loved him so he wouldn't harm us." That's not love; that's fear!! People worship evil dictators under the pretence of "love", because if they didn't, they'd be killed, or banished to die of hardship in inhumane prisons! Is that who God is to you?! Has God been reduced to the lowly status of a human dictator?!

2 Timothy 1:7 (KJV) "For God hath not given us the spirit of fear; but of power, and of love, and of a sound mind." God is to be reverenced, not feared!

There are a world full of reasons for people to actually love God without the fear of consequences, judgment, and punishment; that's what Jesus came to show us, and it's up to us to show others. However, you have to get past whatever it is that hinders you; whether it be ignorance, pride, prejudice, hate, anger, or (God forbid) all of the above!

Many pharisaic people are angered by the fallen nature of humanity (particularly within themselves), so they judge people by their behaviour; rather than seeing them through the eyes of a God of compassion and grace who; in spite of people's behaviour, and without requirement of penance or

A Message to the Self-Righteous

even an apology; allowed His Son to be sacrificed on our behalf, so that we may be reconciled with God; even though our sinful nature remains within us. No matter who we are, or what we've done; the only thing God requires of any of us is our belief in the crucifixion and resurrection of Jesus Christ for our salvation; the Holy Spirit will do the rest, according to the access we give Him.

Let's talk about the LGBTQ community; since they seem to be the favourite target for people who hate on others, whilst professing to be Christians. Do you think they will all burn in hell? Do you think Jesus discriminates; seeing anyone differently than anyone else? NEWS FLASH! **Romans 3:23 (KJV) "For all have sinned, and come short of the glory of God."** It's written in Romans 3:22 that the righteousness of God is meant for all who believe, "for there is no difference"! Neither is there any distinction with regards to sin with God, who says, to break one single law, is as bad as breaking them all! **James 2:10 (Amp). "For whosoever keeps the Law as a whole but stumbles and offends in one single instance has become guilty of breaking all of it."** From the moment the sun rises, to when it sets; there is nothing we of ourselves can do, or not do, that qualifies any of us for access to heaven! **Ephesians 2:8-9 (Amp) [8] "For it is by free grace (God's unmerited favour) that you are saved (delivered from judgment and made partakers of Christ's salvation) through your faith. And** *this salvation is not of yourselves of your own doing, it came not through your own striving, but it is the gift of God;"*

[9] "Not because of works not the fulfilment of the Law's demands, lest any man should boast. It is not the result of what anyone can possibly do, so no one can pride himself in it or take glory to himself." Remove the salvation of Jesus from the equation and we all perish; all of us!!

So who are you to suggest that the LGBTQ community cannot claim salvation unless they "change"?! Did you "change" before you accepted Christ or did God accept you as you are? Are you saying Jesus' sacrifice on the cross is so limited in power that it can only save the (as you call) "good" people?! Even if you did change your ways before you came to Christ, do you really think that's what qualifies you entry into heaven?! No!! **Romans 5:8 (Amp) *"But God shows and clearly proves His own love for us by the fact that while we were still sinners, Christ (the Messiah, the Anointed One) died for us."*** Anyone, absolutely anyone who accepts the gift of eternal life through Jesus Christ, will be received by God, and as for those who haven't; (if the Holy Spirit truly lives within us) we should love them just-as-they-are! **Romans 13:8 (KJV)** *"Owe no man any thing, but to love one another: for he that loveth another hath fulfilled the law."*

As I write this, "Christians" are giving Kanye West a hard time simply because he has invited Jesus Christ into

A Message to the Self-Righteous

his life! Have you guys lost your minds?! What, because he's a celebrity?! What, because he's wealthy?! ***1 Timothy 2:4 (KJV) "Who will have all men to be saved, and to come unto the knowledge of the truth."*** Oh I see, you think Kanye was so bad and you're so good, and God accepts you because you're so "good". Since when do you get to re-write the Word and will of God?! ***Romans 3:10 (KJV) "As it is written, There is none righteous, no, not one." Romans 3:23 (KJV) "For all have sinned, and come short of the glory of God."***

So what do you think qualifies you to enter into heaven? Your good works? Your good behaviour? Because of how much you pray? Because of how loud you shout when you praise or worship God? Because you pay tithes and offerings? If you think it's any of these things then you insult the sacrifice of Jesus on the cross, and you will surely be the person to whom God will say, "I never knew you..." (Mat 7:23).

The thief on the cross was still a thief when Jesus said to him, "this day you will be with me in paradise." (Luke 23:43) The thief didn't jump off the cross, join a church, change his ways, or do good deeds for several years, so he can be accepted by God; he wasn't even baptised! No, he was a thief! A thief that believed Jesus was the saviour of humanity, and on that very same day, he went to heaven; by faith in Jesus, and that faith alone! Kanye West's and any other person's relationship with Jesus (rich, poor, famous or anonymous, gay or straight) is between them and God alone, and we should celebrate and give God praise anytime absolutely anyone says yes to the calling of Jesus Christ!

It is the will of God that all humanity is saved and it is the goodness of God that leads us all to repentance! **Romans 2:1-4 (Amp) [1] "Therefore you have no excuse or defence or justification, O man, whoever you are who judges and condemns another. For in posing as judge and passing sentence on another, you condemn yourself, because you who judge are habitually practicing the very same things that you censure and denounce." [2] "But we know that the judgment (adverse verdict, sentence) of God falls justly and in accordance with truth upon those who practice such things."**

[3] "And do you think or imagine, O man, when you judge and condemn those who practice such things and yet do them yourself, that you will escape God's judgment and elude His sentence and adverse verdict?"

[4] "Or are you so blind as to trifle with and presume upon and despise and underestimate the wealth of His kindness and forbearance and long-suffering patience? Are you unmindful or actually ignorant of the fact that God's kindness is intended to lead you to repent (to change your mind and inner man to accept God's will)?"

These verses (Romans 2:1-4) reveal the heart of God as relating to our attitude towards all of humanity. When God

A Message to the Self-Righteous

talks about you doing the same things as those you accuse, God is saying that from His perspective, there is no distinction between your fallen nature and the fallen nature of those you accuse (judge). Jesus puts it this way: **Matthew 7:1-5 (Amp) [1] "DO NOT judge and criticise and condemn others, so that you may not be judged and criticised and condemned yourselves."**

[2] "For just as you judge and criticise and condemn others, you will be judged and criticised and condemned, and in accordance with the measure you use to deal out to others, it will be dealt out again to you." [3] "Why do you stare from without at the very small particle that is in your brother's eye but do not become aware of and consider the beam of timber that is in your own eye?" [4] "Or how can you say to your brother, Let me get the tiny particle out of your eye, when there is the beam of timber in your own eye?" [5] "You hypocrite, first get the beam of timber out of your own eye, and then you will see clearly to take the tiny particle out of your brother's eye."

Do not misunderstand these words in Matthew 7:1-5; Jesus is not saying that there could possibly come a time (when you "get the beam of timber out of your own eye") that you will be able to criticise and condemn others - no! Our corrupt, fallen nature, that Jesus paid a heavy price for, will forever be a big chunk of wood in our eyes! Do you really think you have the power to remove humanity's sinful nature?! The best we can do is to love people and let our lives be the beacon that leads them to Jesus; the Holy Spirit will take it from there. Even for those who reject God, the same applies, for we are commanded to owe no one anything but to love them (Romans 13:8).

And don't go quoting Romans 1:18-32, trying to make your case against the LGBTQ community, those scriptures apply to ANYONE who rejects God - LGBTQ or straight, rich or broke, or busted and disgusted; white, black, brown, yellow, green, purple or blue! No matter who we are, if we reject God; He simply says to us, "Okay, you won't listen me or acknowledge me, so have at it then", and God gives us over to our own lusts and desires, and by virtue of the spiritual laws relating to the corrupted human spirit; corruption will consume itself. Corruption of itself is destructive. How many parents do you know who've said to their child, "You won't listen to me, so go ahead, do your thing", and they leave the child to their own devices; however, they still love the child. It grieves the Holy Spirit when we are consumed by our own lusts. God is not stupid, He knew what humanity was like; yet He still allowed His Son to die for us. Only love does that! So your hate and condemnation does not represent the heart of God towards humanity.

So you say, what about God's wrath? The wrath of God spoken of in Romans 1:18, is simply the self destruction we

A Message to the Self-Righteous

bring upon ourselves, because the demonic spirit (which is at the root of all unrighteousness) opposes God, and His righteousness, and it seeks to destroy God's creation; humanity in particular. The corrupt, fallen nature of humanity is exploited by the devil (Lucifer) whom God expelled from heaven, and the devil has been busy killing God's creation ever since. How? By simply seducing humanity with the things that appeal to our flesh. Like I said in chapter 15: our flesh is not our friend, so all the devil does is present opportunities in this fallen world (which we are exposed to everyday) that appeal to our flesh, and when we embrace them; rather than reject them, we reap the self destructive consequences.

Isaiah 54:8-10 (KJV) [8] "In a little wrath I hid my face from thee for a moment; but with everlasting kindness will I have mercy on thee, saith the Lord thy Redeemer. [9] For this is as the waters of Noah unto me: for as I have sworn that the waters of Noah should no more go over the earth; so have I sworn that I would not be wroth with thee, nor rebuke thee. [10] For the mountains shall depart, and the hills be removed; but my kindness shall not depart from thee, neither shall the covenant of my peace be removed, saith the Lord that hath mercy on thee."

My point is, God is not angry with humanity. How can He be? He gave His beloved Son to die on our behalf - everyone; not just you, or the people you like! Don't be naive,

God loved you before you became a Christian! You do realise that don't you?! ***Romans 5:8 (KJV) "But God commended His love toward us, in that, while we were yet sinners, Christ died for us."*** This means that if the people described in Romans 1:18-32, whom God gave over to their own lust, decide to (if possible) change their mind (not their ways!) and accept God into their lives; they will be forgiven - just-as-they-are!! So if we simply offer (not force) our guidance, and extend our love and support, the Holy Spirit will do the rest - that's His job!

So what then, should we not call anybody out on their behaviour? Of course we should! I'm calling you out now, and Jesus did, when He rebuked the Scribes, and the Pharisees, and when he rebuked the money changers and vendors at the temple! Our motives; however, for calling people out, should be our love for those who are being misled, and righteous indignation towards those who are misleading them. Call people out by all means, but in the spirit of love, and for the preservation of the gospel of grace; but not via the spirit of judgment and condemnation, or the spirit of iniquity; even if they declare themselves your enemy. ***Rom12:17-21 (KJV) [17] "Recompense to no man evil for evil. Provide things honest in the sight of all men. [18] If it be possible, as much as lieth in you, live peaceably with all men. [19] Dearly beloved, avenge not yourselves, but rather give place unto wrath: for it is written, Vengeance is mine; I will repay, saith the Lord. [20] Therefore***

A Message to the Self-Righteous

if thine enemy hunger, feed him; if he thirst, give him drink: for in so doing thou shalt heap coals of fire on his head. [21] Be not overcome of evil, but overcome evil with good." Whilst we're on the subject, If this is expected of us concerning those who declare themselves as our enemies, how much more should we seek to show the love, goodness, compassion, and grace of God; not just towards Christians, but anyone we preach the gospel to, who may simply be curious about seeking a relationship with God.

Notwithstanding, Rom 12:17-21 does not mean support or encourage the behaviour of those who do evil, or declare them your enemies, instead you should pray for their deliverance. *1 Timothy 2:1-5 (KJV) "I exhort therefore, that, first of all, supplications, prayers, intercessions, and giving of thanks, be made for all men; [2] For kings, and for all that are in authority; that we may lead a quiet and peaceable life in all godliness and honesty. [3] For this is good and acceptable in the sight of God our Saviour; [4] Who will have all men to be saved, and to come unto the knowledge of the truth. [5] For there is one God, and one mediator between God and men, the man Christ Jesus."* Every human being (not just the ones you like) is precious in God's eyes; therefore, we should give thanks for all whom we pray for; whether they be kings, presidents, anyone in authority, or otherwise; as we are all God's creation, and it's God's desire for all of us to be saved from destruction.

You cannot pray effectively for anyone without giving thanks to God for them. "Giving thanks for the person you're praying for." This is where a lot of people would get off the bus! Oh, you're happy to pray for them; but give thanks?! Now that's painful for some! Someone's behaviour ruffles your feathers, or at worst, causes you harm, and God wants you to give thanks for them?! God; however, is wise (and has a sense of humour), because He knows that for you to give thanks to God for someone who may have caused you grief, or even harm; requires you to deeply immerse yourself into the spirit of righteousness (the Holy Spirit), so that you may take on the true character of Jesus Christ. This process alone makes you bigger, greater and more powerful in Christ; giving you greater depth of spiritual vision, which of course then spills over into every aspect of your life; including your attitude towards humanity as a whole.

So how, for example, should you pray (giving thanks) for someone like United States President, Donald Trump? This is an individual who is in the best position to lead the charge in uniting the country, and dare I say the world, yet he repeatedly lashes out at people who disagree with him through statements and comments that clearly are not motivated by love, compassion, or unity. There are people, including Christians, supporting his behaviour as if he were their god. This is not good, and our Sovereign Almighty God

A Message to the Self-Righteous

is not pleased. So how should you pray? It's not about giving thanks for what Donald Trump says or does; instead, it's about giving thanks that he's a vessel in a position of power that God could use for good. So your prayer should be that God would surround Donald Trump with people who possess the love, grace, and boldness of Jesus; who (because of their unconditional love) have God given authority to speak truth to power. Is there any amongst us?! You should also pray that God would continually bombard Donald Trump's conscience with all things honourable, truthful and decent. That being said; regardless of how much you pray, ultimately it's up to Donald Trump to humble himself before God. It's up to Donald Trump to embrace and to lean into righteousness, and abhor evil.

At some point, Donald Trump will reap that which he has sown (good or evil); but that's God's business, not ours. You; however, should pray that President Trump would (by example) encourage decency, kindness, honesty and unity amongst all Americans, and not just those who express support for him. Not only will the people of the United States benefit; but he would set an example for leaders the world over, which would truly be a great legacy. This is the true measure of Donald Trump's character; but is anyone telling him that?! For those closest to him (including Christians) who are not; woe be unto you, for God will hold you accountable!

Oh yes, you could pray for God to punish Donald Trump. You could pray that he be totally humiliated in some way; however, the vengeance of God is something you should never desire for anyone; even those who declare themselves your enemies. ***Proverbs 24:17 (Amp) "Rejoice not when your enemy falls, and let not your heart be glad when he stumbles or is overthrown."*** Why? Because that means the devil has gotten a victory over a soul for whom Jesus was sacrificed, and we should never want to give the devil a win, no matter whose soul it is; however, know this: it is an insult to all that Jesus stands for (of whom you say you are disciples) when Christians offer prayers supporting the behaviour of anyone in authority (or otherwise), who (with forethought) willingly, deliberately and intentionally gives life to wickedness. ***Proverbs 24:24-25 (KJV) [24] "He that saith unto the wicked, Thou art righteous; him shall the people curse, nations shall abhor him. [25] But to them that rebuke him shall be delight, and a good blessing shall come upon them."*** Verse 24 is referring to people (like the Scribes and Pharisees) who willingly, deliberately and intentionally give life to wickedness; who, with forethought, knowingly reject truth and the goodness of God for their own personal gain, and to the detriment of others. These people are "The wicked" Proverbs 24:24 is referring to and they should not be praised as being righteous!

A Message to the Self-Righteous

Compared to God and compared to what we were created to be before the fall of Adam and Eve; all of humanity is wicked. Not by choice, but by default because of the fall; however, in spite of our imperfections, people generally try to do good. By contrast, there are those who wilfully choose to be wicked, and deliberately yield to and embrace their darker nature; adversely affecting the lives of those around them.

When we consider that compared to God, we are all wicked; we should be careful not to consider well meaning people as "The wicked" referred to in Proverbs 24:24-25.

As I said, generally, people desire to do good; however, there are those who wilfully, and with forethought, choose to do evil to the detriment of others, and for their own personal gain. So when you lash out judgment and condemnation ("fire and brimstone") against those whom Jesus sacrificed His life to save (which by the way is all of humanity), you do a grave injustice to the gospel of grace.

Now if you feel "picked on", or as some people like to say, "feel a prick in your spirit" from reading this chapter; then that's probably because you yourself are self righteous; however, that doesn't necessarily mean that you are the "wicked" referred to in Proverbs 24; it all depends on the spirit or motives behind your self righteous attitude, as it could be just ignorance. Nonetheless, you should not lash out at well meaning people who are (in the eyes of God) just as flawed as you are; telling them how bad they are. In any case, whether a person is deliberately leaning-in to wickedness, or simply wicked by default (because of the "fall"); our fight is not against people, but against wickedness (evil) itself, which is spiritual. **Ephesians 6:12 (KJV) *"For we wrestle not against flesh and blood, but against principalities, against powers, against the rulers of the darkness of this world, against spiritual wickedness in high places."*** This scripture explains why when Peter (a disciple of Jesus) opposed the idea of Jesus being crucified (Matthew 16:23); Jesus replied, "get behind me Satan"! Jesus wasn't speaking to Peter; He was addressing the spirit behind what Peter was saying! It would've been unfortunate if poor Peter didn't realise this, because his hair would've caught fire (so to speak), bless him.

But seriously, do not think for one moment that God is pleased when you misrepresent the gospel of grace. For those of you who profess to be Christians; at no time should your attitude towards people conflict with or contradict the character and nature of Jesus; never! Jesus did not lash out with criticism and condemnation at the woman who was caught committing adultery (John 8:1-11). He didn't even call her wicked! He said to her, "where are your accusers?" Then He said, "Neither do I condemn you; go, and sin no more." "Go, and sin no more." That's it! That was the rebuke! Jesus didn't say, sin no more or else…! By contrast, Jesus railed

A Message to the Self-Righteous

(criticised and condemned) heavily against the Scribes and Pharisees (Mat 23:1-39), calling them vipers; as well as implying that they've got no chance of escaping the punishment of hell! Wow!!

What's the difference here? Why did Jesus respond differently to the woman who committed adultery, compared to the Scribes and Pharisees? The behaviour of both can be construed as wicked right? The difference is: the woman succumbed to human weakness; a sin we all are guilty of, in some form or another (there is no difference with God). She succumbed to her fallen nature, which gives rise to sin; the sin for which Jesus was sent as an atonement, that the woman (and all of humanity) may be forgiven. Whereas, the Scribes and Pharisees portrayed themselves as holy because of their perceived adherence to the Laws of God (the Law which consequently makes them guilty); purporting to be righteous and superior to those under their authority; whilst deliberately condemning, deceiving, and keeping in spiritual bondage (for the purpose of personal gain) those who trusted them for spiritual leadership; to guide them in spiritual truth and understanding. For such (unless they repent) there is no redemption (Matthew 23:33). Do not pass go, do not collect $200.

So you see, as Jesus demonstrates with the Scribes and Pharisees; it's not always about making "nicey-nicey";

instead, you must be so full of the unconditional love, wisdom and grace of God that you'll know, in any given situation, how you should respond, and so that your response may be "filtered" through (sanctioned by) the Holy Spirit; instead of your flesh. You who are self righteous; however, have taken the word "rebuke" and have filtered it through your fallen nature which is not righteous, harbours condemnation, and craves vengeance and punishment; therefore, with your misguided rebukes of judgment and condemnation, you drive away the very souls that the grace of the Cross was meant to deliver! Yet you praise those who are clearly wicked!

If you are a follower of Christ, your rebuke should be consistent with His nature, and you should never make a well meaning person feel condemned, a well meaning person who is constantly bombarded with the trappings of a fallen world; full of enticements to please their flesh. As I said, our fight is not against those for whom Jesus gave His life and was resurrected, but against wicked forces in the spirit realm. So stop bashing people with threats of hell fire!

It is said that "misery loves company", so there are those who welcome (even upon themselves) your words of judgment and condemnation, because they themselves feel condemned, guilty, and unworthy. However, if you're to be consistent with the character and nature of Christ, you should show grace towards those who are simply lost, and you should call out

A Message to the Self-Righteous

those who are deliberately and deceitfully wicked (as Jesus did with the Scribes and Pharisees); but ultimately your prayer should be that we all humble ourselves before God, accept the salvation of Christ, and simply love one another, because all of us have fallen short of the goodness and glory of God. There are none of us who are righteous of ourselves! There are none who are innocent! Let us; therefore, praise God for His grace through Jesus Christ!

So don't be deceived; if the motivation of your heart towards people (no matter who they are) is inconsistent with the character and personality of Christ (who is the personification of wisdom, unconditional love, grace, patience, mercy and forgiveness), and you are constantly reminding well meaning people about how much they need Jesus because they're so "bad"; then you grieve the Holy Spirit, and my heart weeps for you.

A true spirit of excellence is demonstrated when absolutely everything you do, is done well; not just the things you like.

CHAPTER 17

That's All Folks!

The gospel is a gospel of grace and forgiveness. The misteachings, misconceptions and misinterpretations of the gospel, throughout history and even now in modern times; continue to be driven in part by the lack of understanding, and (more often and more insidiously) in part by the desire to usurp the will of the individual; stemming from greed, malice and the lust for power. The truth is, Jesus came to set us free; but it is completely up to you to believe it and receive it.

I hope what you've come to understand from reading this book, is that God truly respects and honours your free will, and that in truth, the gospel (the good news regarding your salvation through

Christ), which represents God's new covenant with humanity; is like a letter from God that reveals how much He truly loves you. God will not force salvation upon you; you have the free will to choose it. My prayer is that you will see the New Testament teachings that represent the gospel of grace as humanity's recalibration manual, that resets us to our former glory before the "fall"; a second chance, and by an act of your own free will, accept it; so that those around you and whomever you may encounter may benefit from your Godly wisdom, selflessness and new righteous nature that will be yours as a result of your freewill choice.

Thank you for reading this book, I really hope it's helped you in some way. Revealing the truth of the gospel has been a passion of mine for many years, so whenever I'm having a conversation with someone, it doesn't take long before the conversation migrates over to spiritual things. This was no exception whenever I had a conversation with my son-in-law, Dr. Efe Egharevba; the husband of my oldest daughter, Tonisha. In the early days of first meeting Efe, every time we spoke we wouldn't be two minutes into our conversation before I was preaching to him! One day he said to me, "You should write a book! Call it, Therman Sermons!" Now I know he said it just to shut me up; but what I heard was God telling me that there was a book in me! So if anyone ever says to you, "You should write a book!"; there just might be a book in you...or maybe they just want you to shut up.

Printed in Great Britain
by Amazon